MILESTONES IN MODERN WORLD HISTORY

1600 ··· 1750 ···   ··· 1940 ··· 2000

The Battle of Britain

MILESTONES IN MODERN WORLD HISTORY

1600 · · · 1750 · · ·   1940 · · · 2000

The Age of Enlightenment

The Algerian War

The Battle of Britain

The Boer War

The Bolshevik Revolution

The British Industrial Revolution

The Chinese Cultural Revolution

The Collapse of the Soviet Union

The Congress of Vienna

The Cuban Revolution

D-Day and the Liberation of France

The End of Apartheid in South Africa

The Establishment of the State of Israel

The French Revolution and the Rise of Napoleon

The Great Irish Famine

The Indian Independence Act of 1947

The Iranian Revolution

The Manhattan Project

The Marshall Plan

The Mexican Revolution

The Mexican War of Independence

The Perry Expedition and the Opening of Japan

The Protestant Reformation

The Thirty Years' War

The Tiananmen Square Protests

The Treaty of Nanking

The Treaty of Versailles

The Universal Declaration of Human Rights

MILESTONES IN MODERN WORLD HISTORY

The Battle of Britain

ALAN ALLPORT

CHELSEA HOUSE
An Infobase Learning Company

The Battle of Britain

Copyright © 2012 by Infobase Learning

All rights reserved. No part of this book may be reproduced or utilized in any form or by any means, electronic or mechanical, including photocopying, recording, or by any information storage or retrieval systems, without permission in writing from the publisher. For information, contact:

Chelsea House
An imprint of Infobase Learning
132 West 31st Street
New York, NY 10001

Library of Congress Cataloging-in-Publication Data

Allport, Alan, 1970–
  The Battle of Britain / by Alan Allport.
      p. cm. — (Milestones in modern world history)
  Includes bibliographical references and index.
  ISBN 978-1-60413-920-4 (hardcover)
  1. Britain, Battle of, Great Britain, 1940—Juvenile literature. 2. World War, 1939–1945—Great Britain—Juvenile literature. I. Title.
  D756.5.B7A45 2012
  940.54'211—dc23   2011023053

Chelsea House books are available at special discounts when purchased in bulk quantities for businesses, associations, institutions, or sales promotions. Please call our Special Sales Department in New York at (212) 967-8800 or (800) 322-8755.

You can find Chelsea House on the World Wide Web at http://www.infobaselearning.com.

Text design by Erik Lindstrom
Cover design by Alicia Post
Composition by Keith Trego
Cover printed by Yurchak Printing, Landisville, Pa.
Book printed and bound by Yurchak Printing, Landisville, Pa.
Date printed: June 2012

Printed in the United States of America

All links and Web addresses were checked and verified to be correct at the time of publication. Because of the dynamic nature of the Web, some addresses and links may have changed since publication and may no longer be valid.

CONTENTS

1	War in the Skies	7
2	Hitler's Road to War	18
3	Crisis at Dunkirk	31
4	The Adversaries Prepare	43
5	Eagle Day	55
6	The RAF at Bay	67
7	The Blitz	78
8	Invasion Thwarted	90
9	Their Finest Hour	100

Chronology	111
Timeline	112
Notes	115
Bibliography	116
Further Resources	118
Picture Credits	119
Index	120
About the Author	125

War in the Skies

The Germans were not supposed to come over that day. As dawn broke on that murky second Wednesday in July 1940, the sky over southern England was what pilots called "Harry Clampers"—very dank and drizzly, poor flying weather, not at all summerlike. No doubt some tired men of the Royal Air Force (RAF) took one look out of their barracks windows, saw the morning gloom, and returned gratefully to their bunks, expecting a quiet day of rest after the hectic combat they had recently experienced over France.

By late morning, however, patches of gleaming blue sky had begun to break through over Kent and Sussex, and soon reports began to come in of lone German reconnaissance aircraft probing the English horizon, photographing likely future targets. As RAF interceptors were scrambled, the intruders either fled or were cut down by the machine-gun fire of British Hurricane and Spitfire fighters. These were just preliminary movements, mere probing gestures by the German Air Force, the Luftwaffe. Shortly after noon, the plotters at the top secret Radio Direction Finding (RDF) station at Dover confirmed the news: A large concentration of German aircraft was building just across the English Channel. At the headquarters of RAF Fighter Command's 11 Group in northwest London, which was responsible for the defense of southern England, the signal went out to five defending squadrons: Prepare for massed enemy action.

The target was not on land but at sea: a convoy of merchant ships, code-named "Bread," that was steaming through the English Channel. To attack this enticing prize, the Luftwaffe was dispatching its largest force to date, more than 20 Dornier Do 17 light bombers, defended by an equal number of single-engine Messerschmitt Bf 109s and twin-engine Messerschmitt Bf 110s. The Germans sped northwest toward the convoy, partly obscured from sight by thick tufts of clouds that continued to dot the sky.

Suddenly, a line of charcoal-black bursts broke up the German formation, as the radar-assisted guns of the port of Dover began pounding away at the aerial intruders. As the Luftwaffe pilots veered and shimmied to avoid this deadly anti-aircraft fire, one of the Dornier crewmen yelled a warning into his radio microphone: "Hurricanes!" A whole squadron of RAF fighters came roaring at full speed through the shell bursts, charging straight at the German bombers, their machine guns blazing. The Dorniers scattered in disorder, while their Messerschmitt defenders hurriedly swooped down to intercept the Hurricanes.

What followed was to become a typical scene in the sky above southern England that fateful summer. Pilots careened across the firmament, the metal frames of their aircraft screaming as they dived and banked sharply to escape their pursuers. From the ground, condensation vapor trails could be seen building up, as though the tiny aircraft thousands of feet above

Fascist Europe

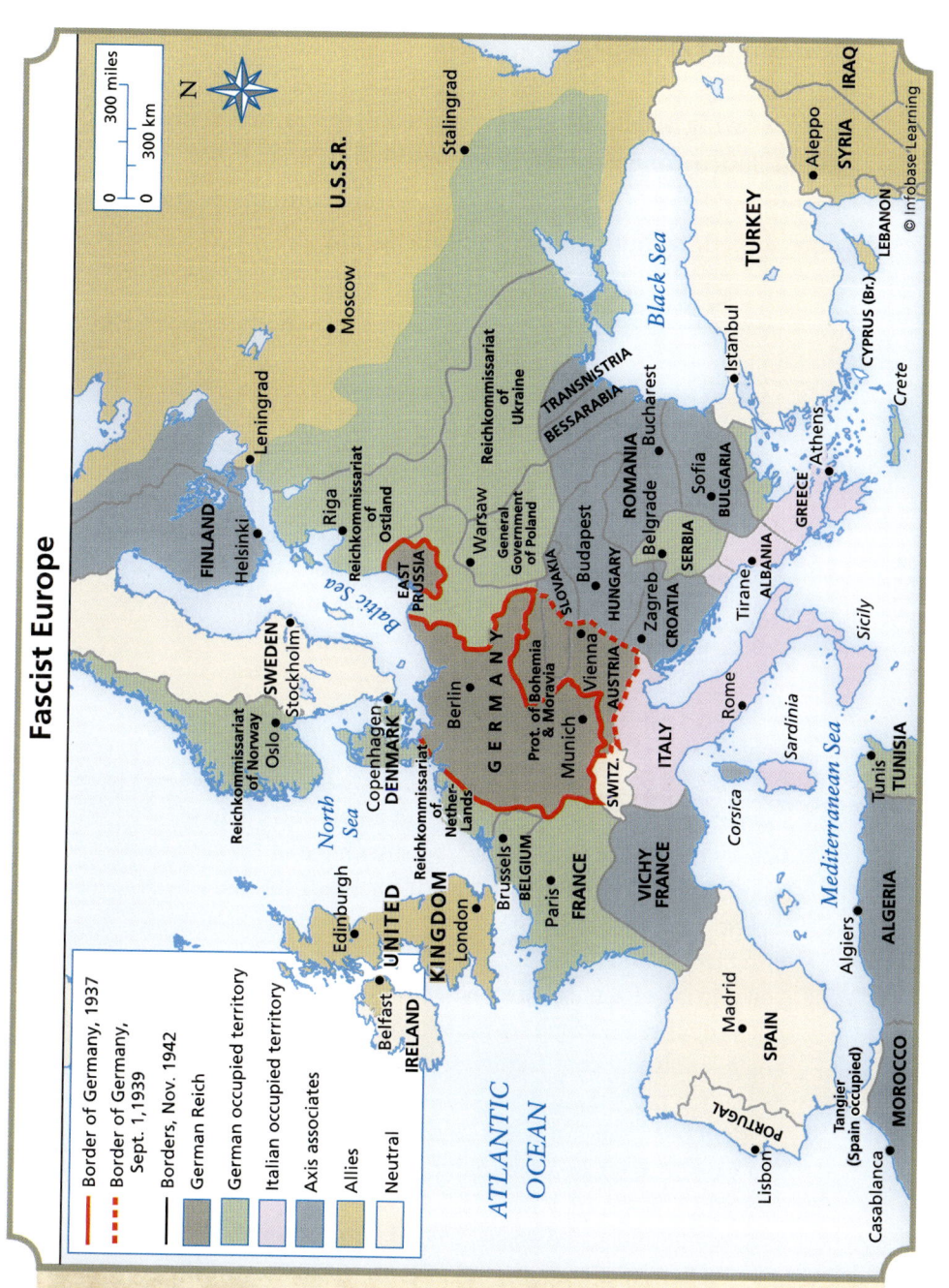

Legend:
- Border of Germany, 1937
- Border of Germany, Sept. 1, 1939
- Borders, Nov. 1942
- German Reich
- German occupied territory
- Italian occupied territory
- Axis associates
- Allies
- Neutral

When Great Britain faced the Nazi war machine in 1940, almost all of Europe had been overrun by Germany and its fascist ally, Italy. This map includes the primary Axis powers, Germany and Italy, the fascist governments they established in France, Poland, Albania, and Greece, and associated fascist states like Hungary, Croatia, and Vichy France. In 1941, both the Soviet Union and the United States would fight alongside Great Britain, but until that time the British would fight alone.

were weaving a delicate tapestry of cobwebs rather than trying to destroy one another. It was an incongruous moment of beauty and death, of technology and nature combining to produce something both graceful and disturbing.

AERIAL COMBAT

Roald Dahl, who later wrote such children's books as *Charlie and the Chocolate Factory* and *Fantastic Mr. Fox*, joined the Royal Air Force as a young man during World War II. Here he describes his first encounter with the enemy:

Suddenly I spotted the bombers. . . . It was my first ever sight of the enemy from my own plane. Quickly I turned the brass ring of my firing button from "safe" to "fire." I switched on my reflector sight and a pale red circle of light with two crossbars appeared suspended in the air in front of my face. I headed straight for the little dots.

Half a minute later, the dots had resolved themselves into black twin-engine bombers. They were Ju 88s. I counted six of them. I glanced above and around them but I could see no fighters protecting them. I remember being absolutely cool and unafraid. My one wish was to do my job properly and not make a hash of it.

I had been warned never to push my throttle "through the gate" except in a real emergency. Going "through the gate" meant that the big Rolls Royce engine would produce absolute maximum revs, and three minutes was the limit of time it could tolerate such stress. OK, I thought, this is an emergency. . . . The engine roared and the Hurricane leaped forward. I began to catch up fast on the bombers. They had now gone into a line-abreast formation which, as I was soon to discover,

War in the Skies

Flying Officer Tom Higgs, a veteran of the peacetime RAF, approached one of the Dorniers in his Hurricane. His bullets scythed into the doomed German bomber. Higgs, however, had gotten too close; as the Dornier desperately weaved to avoid

> allowed all six of their rear-gunners to fire at me simultaneously . . .
>
> I was still gaining on them, and when I was about 200 yards behind them, all six rear-gunners in the Ju 88s began shooting at me. They were using tracer and out of each one of the six rear turrets came a brilliant shaft of orange-red flame arcing towards me. . . . I could see them bending in the air as they came towards me and then suddenly they were flashing past my cockpit like fireworks. . . .
>
> I got a little closer and by jiggling my plane this way and that I managed to get the starboard engine of one bomber into my reflector-sight. I aimed a bit ahead of the engine and pressed the button. The Hurricane gave a small shudder as the eight Brownings in the wings all opened up together, and a second later I saw a huge piece of his metal engine-cowling the size of a dinner plate go flying up into the air. Good heavens, I thought, I've hit him! I've actually hit him! Then black smoke came pouring from the engine and very slowly, almost in slow motion, the bomber winged over to starboard and began to lose height.
>
> I throttled back. He was well below me now. I could see him clearly by squinting down out of my cockpit. . . . He was tumbling slowly over and over like a leaf, the black smoke pouring out. . . . Then I saw one, two, three people jump out of the fuselage and go tumbling earthwards with legs and arms outstretched in grotesque attitudes, and a moment later one, two, three parachutes billowed open and began floating gently down.*
>
> ---
> * Roald Dahl, *Going Solo*. New York: Viking Penguin, 1986.

12 THE BATTLE OF BRITAIN

Seen here, a scene of aerial combat on the Western Front in World War I. By the time of the Battle of Britain a generation later, these fragile aircraft had been replaced by deadlier, faster, and stronger fighters and bombers, capable of crossing the English Channel and unleashing wholesale destruction on cities.

his hail of fire, the planes collided. Higgs's Hurricane, with one of its wings sheared off, spiraled into the English Channel, followed by the wrecked German aircraft. In the confusion, some of his comrades thought they saw Higgs bail out in his parachute. An RAF rescue launch sped to the scene of the floating debris and found two German crewmen still alive. There was no sign of Higgs; his body washed ashore on the Dutch coast two days later.

This day, July 10, 1940, would later be officially recognized as the opening day of the Battle of Britain, and Higgs was the RAF's first combat death. His would eventually be followed by 543 others.

"UPON THIS BATTLE DEPENDS THE SURVIVAL OF CHRISTIAN CIVILIZATION"

That brief dogfight over the English Channel in July 1940 was the preliminary skirmish in what was to become the most momentous aerial conflict in the history of warfare. The Battle of Britain was a three-month assault on England by the Luftwaffe, an assault intended to break the British will to resist and to prepare the way for a land invasion of the United Kingdom. The stakes were clear and terrifying: If the Germans could win the battle, then World War II was over—and Adolf Hitler had won. If the British could prevent that victory, then the war would continue—and the enemies of the Nazi regime would have bought themselves some precious breathing space to prepare their defenses. Winston Churchill, the British prime minister, spelled out the consequences of failure in an eloquent address to Parliament on June 18, 1940:

> Upon this battle depends the survival of Christian civilization.... The whole fury and might of the enemy must very soon be turned on us. Hitler knows that he will have to break us in this Island or lose the war. If we can stand up to him, all Europe may be free and the life of the world may move

forward into broad, sunlit uplands. But if we fail, then the whole world, including the United States, including all that we have known and cared for, will sink into the abyss of a new Dark Age.[1]

WILLIAM "BILLY" FISKE (1911–1940)

Volunteers from dozens of countries came to England in 1940 to join the Royal Air Force and fight in the Battle of Britain. Although the United States was still a neutral country, 10 U.S. citizens fought in the battle; one of the first of them to sacrifice his life—and one of the first Americans to die in World War II—was William "Billy" Fiske.

Fiske was born in Brooklyn, New York, in 1911, the son of a wealthy New England banker. After attending school in Chicago, he traveled to Europe, where he discovered a passion for winter sports. He became an excellent downhill sled racer and was famed for his daredevil descents down the infamously steep "Cresta Run" in St. Moritz, Switzerland, but his greatest love was for bobsledding. Although just 16, Fiske took part in the 1928 Winter Olympics in St. Moritz and won a gold medal driving the five-man U.S. bobsled team, becoming the youngest person ever to win gold in that sport. Four years later, he repeated his triumph at Lake Placid in New York. He was picked to represent the United States a third time at the 1936 Winter Games in Germany, but he declined to take part. Germany was under the dictatorship of Nazi leader Adolf Hitler, and Fiske would not compete in an event that legitimized Hitler's regime. It was that same distaste for Nazi rule that motivated Fiske to join the Royal Air Force at the outbreak

The Battle of Britain was one of the decisive conflicts of the twentieth century, determining the fate of millions across the world for many decades to follow. It was also a key moment in the history of aviation. Ever since the Wright Brothers had

---

of war in 1939; he pretended to be Canadian to avoid problems with his American citizenship.

Fiske was posted to the RAF's 601 Squadron, known as "the Millionaire's Squadron" because of the high number of wealthy and aristocratic young men in its ranks. In between flying practices, its dashing young pilots, dressed in fashionable silks, would play polo on motorbikes and terrorize the neighborhood in their fast sports cars. Those games, however, gave way to deadly combat in the late spring of 1940 as the Germans began their air attacks on British airfields.

On August 16, 1940, Fiske and his comrades scrambled in their Hurricane fighters to intercept a flight of German dive-bombers. During the ensuing dogfight, 601 Squadron shot down eight enemy aircraft, but a German machine gun bullet sliced through Fiske's gas tank and his plane caught fire. He nursed the crippled Hurricane home and made a successful emergency landing back at his base, but his plane exploded on the runway. Fiske died two days later from his injuries. He was 29 years old. He was buried in the village churchyard in Boxton, Sussex; his gravestone reads, "He died for England."

In all, 6,700 American citizens volunteered to fly with the Royal Air Force during World War II, although only a small proportion of them had the means to get to Britain or Canada to actually start pilot training. The RAF formed three all-American Eagle Squadrons, which were eventually transferred to the U.S. Army Air Forces when the United States entered the war in December 1941.

made their first tentative hops into the air at Kitty Hawk, North Carolina, in 1903, people had wondered about the long-term significance of the airplane. Was it essentially an expensive mechanical toy, a fairground gimmick that could give riders the brief thrilling sensation of being airborne, but with little practical usefulness, or would the invention of the airplane ultimately revolutionize human life?

When the First World War broke out in Europe in 1914, there seemed to be only one military use for airplanes: eyes in the sky. The armies of Germany, France, Russia, and Britain marched into battle with observation planes skittering high above them, their pilots seeking out enemy troop movements on the ground below. This reconnaissance work provided valuable intelligence, but it seemed to exhaust the usefulness of the airplane. In 1914, pilots were still flying aircraft that the Wright Brothers would have recognized: flimsy wood-and-fabric contraptions with tiny engines that could barely produce a few dozen horsepower and which puttered along at 50 miles per hour (80 kilometers per hour) or so. Too fragile to carry anything more than a pilot and a passenger, airplanes seemed unlikely to play more than an ancillary role in the battles to come.

All this was to change dramatically during the four years that World War I was fought. Aircraft grew larger, faster, and more powerful. Pilots began to carry firearms into the air to take potshots at one another, and then machine guns and bombs were mounted to the aircraft. Because planes attacked enemy troops and ground installations, anti-aircraft guns had to be developed to defend men and buildings below. The Germans built giant strategic bombers capable of reaching London; the British retaliated and were on the verge of launching massive air strikes against Berlin when the war ended. By the time Germany surrendered in November 1918, air power had become as vital to national defense as land and sea power. The military aircraft had come of age.

During the 1920s and 1930s, as aviation technology improved, strategists began to wonder whether future wars would be fought entirely in the air. What would a battle solely fought with aircraft look like? What would the most successful tactics be? Could one side impose its will on the other using only air power? How would anyone know who had won or lost? These questions were of vital importance to military planners, but they had no answers. It had never been done.

The struggle between the RAF and the Luftwaffe in the summer of 1940, therefore, was critical not just to the outcome of World War II; it was also a strategic experiment on a grand scale, a test of all the theories proposed by air enthusiasts during the preceding decades. "Air power is like poker," an American Air Force commander would later say: "A second-best hand is like none at all."[2] As the two sides braced themselves for battle that fateful July, who held the aces?

Hitler's Road to War

At 20 minutes to five on the morning of Friday, September 1, 1939, a German force of 29 gull-winged Junkers Ju 87 "Stuka" dive-bombers were 15,000 feet (4,572 meters) above the Polish town of Wieluń. At a signal from their commander, the planes suddenly flipped over and dove almost straight toward the ground, their pilots thrown back in their seats by the g-force of the maneuver. As the Stukas plummeted toward Earth at 370 mph (595 kph), each aircraft emitted a horrible wailing sound generated by its so-called Jericho's Trumpet—a hollow wind-driven siren designed to strike fear into spectators on the ground below. It must have seemed that the plunging Stukas would be dashed to pieces any second, but 1,500 feet (457 m) above Wieluń, the leading plane suddenly jerked violently upward and released a large bomb mounted on its undercarriage that continued to plummet to the ground. Soon, other dive-bombers followed one by one.

Wieluń was engulfed in flames as the bombs hit their targets with unnerving precision. By the time the attack was over minutes later, hundreds of the town's citizens were dead or badly injured. Wieluń itself was a smoking ruin, its hospital and historic church reduced to rubble. Few Poles, however, had time that morning to mourn their martyred countrymen for long. All across Poland, German troops and tanks were pouring across the frontier. Without so much as a declaration of war, Germany had suddenly and ruthlessly attacked its eastern neighbor, defying the warnings of the great powers of Europe, Great Britain and France, who weeks before had threatened that such an attack would provoke them to defend Poland with military force. On Sunday, September 3, 1939, having received no answer to their final ultimatum, the two democracies declared war on Germany. World War II had begun. The dead of Wieluń, already forgotten by both sides, would have the dubious distinction of being the first to be killed in a war that would last for six years and see the deaths of at least 50 million people.

THE UNEASY PEACE

How had Europe come to be once again engulfed in war, 21 years after the end of a terrible conflict that at the time had been called "the war to end all wars"? The roots of World War II lay in the unsatisfactory settlement of that previous war and the powerful sense of grievance among those who had fought on the losing side, especially in Germany.

World War I had ended on November 11, 1918. The four-year war between the Allies (principally France, Britain, Russia, and eventually the United States) and the Central Powers (Germany, Austria, and Turkey) had cost more than 16 million lives. Each nation had fought a "total war" effort, meaning that it had mobilized all the resources of its economy—population, wealth, and industrial output—in order to secure victory. Yet victory had proven bittersweet. Although the Allies were able to defeat the Central Powers, they were almost as exhausted in 1918 as the losers. For four years, each nation had poured its accumulated blood and treasure into a series of grueling battles of attrition. Ingenious military weapons—tanks, machine guns, quick-firing artillery, barbed wire, poison gas, and bomber aircraft—had been developed on both sides. Each technological breakthrough, however, only seemed to make a decisive success harder to achieve. For the ordinary soldiers, bogged down in muddy trenches that stretched hundreds of miles across the battlefields of Europe, the experience of the war was one of terrifying futility.

Even in the final months of the war, the outcome seemed uncertain. In 1917, the Bolshevik Revolution broke out in Russia, and the following year the Germans were able to exploit the chaos by forcing the new Russian government to sue for a separate peace. For Germany, ultimate victory seemed in sight. The Allies' loss of Russia, however, was more than compensated for by the decision of President Woodrow Wilson in April 1917 to bring the United States into the war on their side. The U.S. entry into the war tipped the balance in the Allies' favor. By November 1918, the Austrian and Turkish empires had disintegrated and Germany was on the brink of revolution itself. Wilhelm II, the German emperor, abdicated and fled the country, and the country's new republican government requested a cease-fire.

Over the next seven months, the Allied leaders met in Paris to draw up a peace settlement. This agreement, known as the Treaty of Versailles, was approved in June 1919. German envoys, who had not been invited to the negotiations, were summoned to Paris and given an ultimatum: Either sign and accept the terms of the treaty in full or face an immediate resumption of the war. Germany, battered by years of warfare,

British troops go over the top of the trenches during the Battle of the Somme in 1916, during World War I. Germany's defeat in the war led to the rise of Adolf Hitler and his Nazi Party in the interwar years.

was in no condition to continue fighting. With great reluctance, the envoys signed. The war was over.

The treaty's provisions, however, were contradictory. On the one hand, its authors hoped that it would resolve the age-old European disputes that had caused the war in the first place. On the other hand, all the Allied leaders believed strongly that Germany, as the leading member of the Central Powers, had to be punished for its role in the conflict's origins. Germany was forced to give up territory on its western and eastern borders. It was no longer allowed to possess a navy, an air force, or anything more than a token army, and it was required to pay an

(continues on page 24)

ADOLF HITLER (1889–1945)

Because Adolf Hitler's very name has become a byword for evil, it is often hard to remember that for many people in the 1930s (and not just in Germany) Hitler was a hero: His bold seizure of power and his determination to end his country's economic and political troubles made him seem a dynamic and impressive figure. When he became German chancellor in 1933, few people imagined that he would drag the world into a devastating global war that would cause the deaths of 50 million people.

Although his family was German-speaking, Hitler was born in a town in northern Austria rather than in Germany itself. His father, Alois, was a minor customs official in the Austrian civil service and a petty tyrant at home. After his father's early death in 1903, Hitler left school and drifted to the Austrian capital, Vienna, where he spent several years as an unsuccessful art student. After World War I broke out in July 1914, the excited young man traveled to Munich to enlist in a Bavarian infantry regiment. He spent the war in the trenches of the Western Front and was recovering from wounds in a hospital in November 1918 when he heard the news that Germany had surrendered. Devastated, he, like many other disillusioned veterans, blamed the defeat on the supposed treachery of left-wing politicians and Jews on the home front. He became obsessed with punishing his adopted country's "enemies" and restoring Germany to its place as master of Europe.

After leaving the army, Hitler began attending meetings of a fringe right-wing group based in Munich called the National Socialist German Workers Party (NSDAP, or "Nazi" Party for short). He quickly rose to become undisputed leader of the party. In November 1923, an overconfident Hitler led an armed attack against the Bavarian local government, but the attempted revolution was a fiasco and he was sentenced to one year in jail. During his imprisonment, he wrote his famous autobiography and political manifesto, *Mein Kampf* ("My Struggle").

After his failure in Munich, Hitler decided to seek power through the ballot box rather than by violent revolt. The breakthrough came in 1930, after Germany collapsed into economic chaos following the 1929 Wall Street crash. Hitler's seductive promise to restore the country to its former glory appealed to millions of distressed unemployed workers. In the election of July 1932, the Nazis won more votes than any other political party. The following January, President Paul von Hindenberg, reluctantly appointed Hitler chancellor of Germany.

Hitler quickly used his new powers to destroy all opposition to Nazi rule; within 12 months the country was a one-party dictatorship. After Hindenberg died in August 1934, Hitler declared himself *Führer* ("leader") of what he called the Großdeutsches Reich, or the "Greater German Empire." Over the next half-decade, he rebuilt German society according to his own Nazi model, which included the stripping of citizenship from the country's Jewish population. In September 1939, Hitler's invasion of Poland triggered the outbreak of World War II. Almost six years later, on April 30, 1945, having brought his once-mighty empire to overwhelming defeat at the hands of Great Britain, the United States, and the Soviet Union, Hitler killed himself in his command bunker in Berlin.

(continued from page 21)
enormous sum in reparations, or damages, to the Allies for the cost of the war.

Although the Germans managed to avoid repaying more than a token sum of these reparations, the humiliating terms of the "Slave Treaty," as it became known, burned deep into the German people's sense of pride. Many ordinary Germans could not understand why they had lost a war they seemed to be on the verge of winning. They resented the republican government's decision to sign the Treaty of Versailles. Broken by an economy battered by the terms of the treaty and all but dismantled by the Great Depression of the 1930s, the Germans sought a savior, someone to explain the failures of the past and redeem the nation from its suffering. They found it in the person of Adolf Hitler.

HITLER'S NEW GERMANY

Hitler promised Germans a revitalized nation, one that would rise from the ashes of defeat and return to its proper position as the leading nation of Europe. He promised to overthrow the Treaty of Versailles and humble the arrogant Allies. Most of all, he promised to identify and punish the internal enemies of Germany who had caused the nation's defeat in World War I. To Hitler, Germany had lost the war only because of traitors at home. Hitler's traitors came in many guises: socialists, communists, and profiteering businessmen. He believed that they had one thing in common: Their ranks were dominated by Jews. Jewish conspirators, he declared, had been engaged in a decades-long plot to bring down Germany. Hitler and his supporters in the National Socialist German Workers Party (the NSDAP, or "Nazi" Party) would crush the enemy within and restore racial purity to the Fatherland before embarking on a quest for European primacy.

Under normal circumstances, Hitler and the Nazis would probably have remained marginal figures in the political debate.

Hitler's Road to War

Seen here, Adolf Hitler, chancellor of Germany, is welcomed by supporters at Nuremberg, Germany, in 1933. Hitler's message of a resurgent Germany capable of crushing its enemies, both real and imaginary, found a ready audience with many members of a German population beaten down by economic hardships.

The 1920s, however, were not normal times. Germany was bedeviled by economic crises that prevented a return to prewar affluence. In 1923, the hyperinflation of the German currency reduced its value to virtually nothing and wiped out the savings of millions of middle-class families. Then in 1929, the shock wave of the stock market collapse in America sparked the beginning of the Great Depression. Germany was one of the worst affected nations. Unemployment rose to 6 million people. Desperate and angry, Germans lost faith in the moderate political parties. The Nazis ingeniously exploited each crisis for their own ends. By mid-1932, they had become the largest political group in the German parliament. The following year, Hitler was appointed chancellor and promptly began to dismantle the republic's democratic structure using violence and intimidation to silence all dissent. In 1934, he formally abolished the republic and announced the creation of the Third Reich (or "empire").

Most Germans were not concerned about the loss of their personal freedoms so long as the Nazis could return their country to prosperity. At least superficially, Hitler did just that. He poured money into construction projects and, in defiance of the Versailles Treaty, rebuilt the nation's armed forces. These initiatives created jobs for the unemployed. Government spending boosted Germany's gross domestic product (GDP), the leading indicator of economic growth. In the long term, Hitler's policies were probably unsustainable. Nazi Germany could not sell nearly enough exports to pay for the massive amounts of imported raw materials required to maintain its growth rate, and the Third Reich was fast running out of foreign currency reserves to pay for them. Hitler, however, was not concerned. War would neatly solve this problem.

CRISIS AND WAR

Hitler moved slowly at first on the diplomatic stage. He knew that it would take time to build up Germany's armed forces to a level that could seriously challenge the British and French. So he blustered and threatened, but did little. By 1936, however, Hitler was confident enough to begin rolling back the Treaty of Versailles. He announced that German troops would reenter the Rhineland, an area of western Germany bordering France that had been compulsorily demilitarized after World War I. Germany's army commanders were secretly nervous about such a blatant act of provocation, but neither France nor Britain responded. Hitler's audacity had paid off. It seemed safe to push still further.

While the British and French governments did not like Hitler or his regime, they were unsure what to do about

Nazi leader Adolf Hitler beckons to Prime Minister Neville Chamberlain of Great Britain (*center*), during Chamberlain's visit to Munich, which led to the Munich Agreement in September 1938 permitting the Nazi annexation of Czechoslovakia's Sudetenland. From second left are Hitler's interpreter, Paul Schmidt; Chamberlain; the British ambassador to Germany, Nevile Henderson; and the German foreign minister, Joachim von Ribbentrop.

Germany. Both countries had suffered terrible losses in World War I and neither wished to fight another major war unless absolutely necessary. In addition, many people in Britain and France agreed with the Nazis that the terms of the Versailles Treaty had been too harsh. Perhaps, many felt, Hitler's demands were not so unreasonable. Even if Hitler could not be successfully appeased, however, the Allies felt that they needed time to rebuild their armed forces before confronting Germany. If that

(continues on page 30)

APPEASEMENT

In the fall of 1938, Europe found itself on the brink of war when Hitler demanded that Czechoslovakia hand over its western border region, known as the Sudetenland, to Germany. The British and French governments initially backed Czechoslovakia, but at a last-minute crisis meeting in Munich on September 29 (to which the Czechs were not invited), they agreed to appease the German demands and compel their ally to give way. The so-called Munich Agreement was controversial. Many people at the time believed that the issue was too trivial to be worth risking the lives of millions. Prime Minister Neville Chamberlain of Great Britain defended his policy of appeasement in Parliament:

> [Many people] have written to my wife or myself in these last weeks to tell us of their gratitude for my efforts and to assure us of their prayers for my success. . . . It has been heartbreaking to read of the growing anxiety they reveal and their intense relief when they thought, too soon, that the danger of war was past.
>
> If I felt my responsibility heavy before, to read such letters has made it seem almost overwhelming. How horrible, fantastic, incredible it is that we should be digging trenches and trying on gas masks here because of a quarrel in a far-away country between people of whom we know nothing. . . .
>
> I can well understand the reasons why the Czech Government have felt unable to accept the terms which have been put before them in the German memorandum . . . [but] however much we may sympathize with a small nation confronted by a big and powerful neighbor, we cannot in all circumstances undertake to involve the whole

British Empire in war simply on her account. . . . War is a fearful thing, and we must be very clear, before we embark upon it, that it is really the great issues that are at stake, and that the call to risk everything in their defense, when all the consequences are weighed, is irresistible.*

Others, however, felt that the Munich Agreement was a cynical betrayal that would only encourage Hitler to make further demands. Winston Churchill, leader of the anti-appeasers in Parliament, made a powerful speech condemning Chamberlain's actions:

We have sustained a total and unmitigated defeat. . . . Do not let us blind ourselves to that. . . .
  I do not grudge our loyal, brave people, who were ready to do their duty no matter what the cost, who never flinched under the strain of last week. I do not grudge them the natural, spontaneous outburst of joy and relief when they learned that the hard ordeal would no longer be required of them at the moment; but they should know the truth. . . . They should know that we have passed an awful milestone in our history, when the whole equilibrium of Europe has been deranged. . . .
  And do not suppose that this is the end. This is only the beginning of the reckoning. This is only the first sip, the first foretaste of a bitter cup which will be proffered to us year by year unless by a supreme recovery of moral health and martial vigour, we arise again and take our stand for freedom as in the olden time.**

---

*Neville Chamberlain, *In Search of Peace*. New York, G. P. Putnam's Sons, 1939, p. 393.
** Winston Churchill, "A Total and Unmitigated Defeat," speech given to the House of Commons, October 5, 1938. http://www.churchill-society-london.org.uk/Munich.html.

(continued from page 27)

meant temporarily buying off Hitler with the territory of other nations until they were ready to challenge him, then so be it. It was a cynical policy, but it was not irrational under the very difficult circumstances they found themselves in.

This helps to explain why Britain and France did not initially react to Germany's provocations. In 1938, Hitler defied the Versailles Treaty again by annexing Austria and demanding a large slice of Czechoslovakia populated by German-speaking people. The leaders in London and Paris hoped that these concessions would keep Hitler satisfied for the time being. In March 1939, however, the Nazis blatantly ignored the promises they had made a year earlier to stop expanding German territory when they occupied the rest of Czechoslovakia. Now nothing but force seemed likely to deter Hitler. Poland looked to be the Germans' next target. Britain and France pledged to defend Poland and warned Hitler that any further aggression would mean immediate attack. Assuming they were bluffing, Hitler went ahead anyway and invaded Poland on September 1, 1939. It was no bluff. Two days later, Europe was at war.

Though no one could have predicted it at the time, less than a year after the destruction of Wieluń, German aircraft would be over French and British towns raining destruction on their inhabitants.

Crisis at Dunkirk

On October 6, 1939, the last isolated Polish garrisons still resisting the Germans surrendered. It had taken Hitler's forces a little more than a month to defeat their eastern neighbor. Poland's army had fought bravely, but the outcome of the battle had been all but preordained. This was for three reasons.

First, the Polish forces were large but technologically obsolete. Poland could mobilize about 1 million soldiers, but most of them were equipped with World War I-era weapons; they had relatively few tanks and relied for mobility mainly on the horse rather than the truck. The Polish Air Force trained its pilots well, but its aircraft were largely out of date, and the German attack arrived so suddenly that many planes were destroyed on the ground before they could take off. The Germans had numerical superiority over the Poles on land

and in the air, and more importantly their weapons and tactics were more suited to a modern fast-paced war of movement. Germany possessed 3,000 tanks organized into six armored (or *Panzer*) divisions. These were specially trained to break through the opposing side's front line and rapidly advance into the enemy hinterland, cutting lines of supply and communication and spreading panic in their wake. The Panzers were supported from the air by Stuka dive-bombers acting as "flying artillery," able to knock out vital points of resistance with precision accuracy. The new style of warfare practiced so effectively by the Germans in Poland was dubbed *Blitzkrieg*, or "lightning war."

The second reason for Poland's defeat was that the Soviet Union also invaded Poland from the east on September 17. This shocked the world; Soviet leader Joseph Stalin's communist government had never made any secret of its hatred for Nazi Germany, and the feeling was mutual. Stalin, however, also distrusted Britain and France and suspected (with some good reason) that the two western democracies would be happy to stand on the sidelines while Hitler attacked the USSR. So Stalin had decided in the summer of 1939 to cut a deal with Hitler and buy his country some time and security. The two adversaries agreed to divide Poland between them. The Soviet Union's invasion left Poland's forces totally surrounded and their strategic position hopeless.

Finally, Poland was doomed because Britain and France did nothing to help their ally. This was not so much out of a lack of willingness to help as an inability to do so. Both countries had planned for a defensive war against Germany, assuming that the Germans would immediately attack France on the outbreak of war as they had done in 1914. It had never seriously occurred to the military planners of either country that they might have to go on the offensive at the start of a future war against Hitler, especially to help a country hundreds of miles from their own borders. Their armies were neither trained nor equipped to launch such an ambitious attack. So they sat and waited instead. It was an understandable decision under the circumstances. By handing Germany the initiative in this way, however, the British and French had sown the seeds of their own destruction nine months later.

THE PHONY WAR

After Poland surrendered, the war entered a peculiar state of inactivity. The British and the French dug in on the border with Germany and continued to wait for something to happen. The Germans, who needed to rest and reequip their army and air force after the Polish campaign, were in no immediate hurry to attack. So throughout the winter of 1939 and 1940, there was virtually no fighting at all. This became known as the "Phony War," or, to the Germans, the *Sitzkrieg*: the sitting war. Occasionally the Allies would fly a few bombers over a German city to drop leaflets urging their enemy to surrender immediately. Not surprisingly, this did not produce very effective results.

Not everyone on the Allied side was so passive. At the outbreak of war, Winston Churchill had been appointed First Lord of the Admiralty, the man who commanded Britain's mighty Royal Navy. He continually agitated for more action against the Germans. One of his ideas was a preemptive move against Norway. Because the northern Baltic Sea froze in the winter, the Germans had to ship crucial iron-ore imports from Sweden along the Norwegian coastline instead. Churchill wanted to mine these waters to stop the German ships and disrupt Germany's economy. Like a lot of Churchill's ideas, it was ingenious but not all that well thought-out. It would be legally questionable—Norway was, after all, neutral—but more importantly it did not address what the British and French should do if Germany responded to this provocation.

In any case, the British government dithered over Churchill's proposal and did not decide to go ahead until the spring of 1940, by which time Hitler had gotten wind that something was about to happen in Scandinavia. Deciding to act first, the Germans launched a sudden strike against Norway on April 9, taking Oslo with little resistance. They also occupied Denmark

WINSTON CHURCHILL (1874–1965)

At the outbreak of World War II, Winston Churchill was a respected and experienced politician but also a man who appeared to be on the brink of his retirement. At 64 years old, it did not seem likely that Churchill would play a very major role in the conflict to come. By a remarkable and largely accidental series of events, however, Churchill became not only prime minister of Great Britain at its hour of greatest crisis but also the great champion of the western democracies in their struggle against Hitler. A soldier, journalist, author, and painter as well as a statesman, Churchill remained even in old age a man of incredible vigor and a boundless curiosity for life.

Churchill was born into a distinguished aristocratic family. His father, Lord Randolph Churchill, was an important politician in the Conservative Party. Churchill's mother, Jennie Jerome, was the Brooklyn-born daughter of a Wall Street financier, giving Churchill a personal link to the United States that would play an important role in his life. His childhood was not happy. Largely overlooked by his parents, who had a whirlwind social life, Churchill was shunted from one boarding school to another. His progress in class was slow, and his teachers were unimpressed. His father regarded him as lazy and feeble-minded.

Churchill did not really shine until he joined the British Army as an officer cadet in 1893. He had many youthful at the same time. An Anglo-French expeditionary force was hurriedly put together and sent to western Norway, but it was poorly equipped and lacked proper air cover. The expedition

---

adventures in the army, fighting in several imperial campaigns and becoming a prisoner-of-war during Britain's conflict with the South African Boers in 1899. After a daring escape from his Boer captors, Churchill returned to Britain, where the fame of his recent exploits helped him win a seat in Parliament. Churchill remained a member of the House of Commons from 1900 until his retirement 63 years later. He had a highly successful early career, playing an important role in the British government during World War I. By the early 1930s, however, Churchill was increasingly seen as old and out of touch. Removed from high political office, he took to writing instead and produced a bestselling memoir of the war and a number of major histories. During this period, Churchill's warnings about the growing threat from Adolf Hitler's Nazi Germany were largely ignored. Even members of his own Conservative Party regarded him as a reckless warmonger.

When war finally did break out again in September 1939, Churchill was appointed to command Britain's Royal Navy. Less than a year later, however, he unexpectedly found himself prime minister when Neville Chamberlain resigned in disgrace. Churchill led Britain to victory in 1945, becoming as famous for his inspiring prose and speeches as he did for his military decision-making. Although defeated by his political opponents near the war's end, Churchill went on to another term as prime minister from 1951 to 1955. At his death in 1965, he was the most famous Englishman in the world and his state funeral was watched on television by millions.

Winston Churchill arrives at 10 Downing Street, the British prime minister's residence, on May 7, 1940, the day Prime Minister Neville Chamberlain resigned in disgrace. Churchill replaced Chamberlain as prime minister.

soon found itself hemmed in and was eventually forced to evacuate Norway in disarray.

In Britain, the main result of the Norwegian campaign was political. Neville Chamberlain had been a lackluster and uninspiring war leader, and the failure in Norway seemed to encapsulate everything that was wrong in his government. In the debate on the campaign in the House of Commons at the beginning of May, many members of his own party criticized him. It quickly became clear that his position was untenable. The man who benefited most from this was the same man who had dreamed up the Norwegian expedition in the first place: Churchill. Chamberlain resigned on May 10, 1940, and Churchill was appointed prime minister in his place. It was, in many ways, a strange decision. Churchill was not particularly trusted or even liked by many of his colleagues. Unlike most other politicians at the time, however, he seemed to have a will to win the war—to do *something* rather than just sit back. He was a risk, but a risk worth taking.

THE GERMANS STRIKE

There was no honeymoon period for Churchill. On the same day that he was appointed prime minister, the Germans—purely by coincidence—finally launched their long-awaited attack against the west. The first blows came in the north against neutral Holland and Belgium. German paratroopers dropped across the Netherlands, quickly seizing the vital bridgeheads across the Rhine estuary. Queen Wilhelmina and her government fled the country for exile in London. The Netherlands surrendered after just four days. In Belgium, meanwhile, the Germans quickly captured a vital fortress at the center of the country's defensive line using glider-borne commandos armed with special explosive charges. Belgian troops fell back, crumbling under the weight of the attack. They appealed urgently for help from Britain and France.

Allied troops marched eastward into Belgium to meet the invading Germans, but the assault on Belgium was a bluff. On

May 13, the real center of the German attack opened up farther south, in the Ardennes forest near Luxembourg. Using combat engineers, the Germans forded the Meuse River and built a pontoon bridge for their tanks. The Ardennes area had never been considered a likely target for the Germans, and the light French defenses collapsed almost immediately. The Panzers crossed the river and headed westward rapidly. If the British and French had kept their heads at this point, it might have been possible to organize a swift counterattack to stem the thin and vulnerable German advance, but panic had already set in. On May 15, Prime Minister Paul Reynaud of France phoned Churchill, saying, "We have been defeated. We are beaten; we have lost the battle."[1] The French had no strategic reserve with which to plug the gap. The battle was over almost before it had begun. The government in Paris began burning its records.

THE MIRACLE OF DUNKIRK

On May 19, German units reached the English Channel at Abbeville. Disturbing reports began to reach the British and French units advancing in Belgium that the Germans were behind them as well as in front of them. Realizing that they were surrounded, they turned around and began to fall back toward the channel ports. Soon, as the seriousness of the situation became clear, the withdrawal turned into a rout: 400,000 men streaming westward in disorder, abandoning all their heavy equipment as they went, constantly harassed by Stukas and other low-flying German aircraft. There seemed to be no way to save this northern army short of surrender. The British and French governments prepared for a catastrophe.

There was one slim possibility. It might be possible to evacuate at least some of the trapped army via the port of Dunkirk. An improvised evacuation scheme began on May 26. Every available vessel, from the largest ocean liner to the tiniest fishing smack, was hastily mustered into service to save the British and French troops. This motley fleet, crewed mostly by

British ships leave Dunkirk crammed with soldiers heading back across the English Channel following the Battle of Dunkirk (May 26–June 4, 1940). With the British Expeditionary Force and other Allied troops pinned down by German forces into a small area around Dunkirk with no hope of escape, the call was made for every ship and boat to leave from Britain to save as many soldiers as possible. Despite the British leaving behind most of their equipment, more than 338,000 Allied troops were brought back to England safely.

civilians, braved mines and Stuka attacks to recover soldiers from the Dunkirk beaches, traveling back and forth across the channel from France to England. In nine days of operations, they managed to evacuate more than 338,000 Allied soldiers from Dunkirk, far more than even the most optimistic planner had ever expected. It was an amazing feat of improvisation and courage. For Britain, it meant that the war was not lost. The army had taken a battering, but it could be rebuilt.

(continues on page 42)

HITLER'S DIRECTIVE: INVADE ENGLAND

On July 16, 1940, Hitler called his most senior military commanders to a special meeting at which he announced Führer Directive 16, a set of instructions outlining Germany's strategic plan for the next stage of the war. Having received no acceptable answer to his peace overtures from the British government, Hitler had decided to prepare for a possible invasion of southern England. As the directive makes clear, a number of preliminary steps would have to be taken before any invasion force could be sent across the English Channel safely:

> *Concerning preparations for an amphibious operation against England. . . .* The purpose of this operation will be to eliminate the English mother country as a base for continuation of the war against Germany and, if it should become necessary, to occupy the entire island.
> To this end I order as follows:
>
> 1. The amphibious operation must be carried out as a surprise crossing on a broad front extending approximately from Ramsgate to the region of the Isle of Wight, with Luftwaffe elements assuming the role of artillery, and naval units assuming the role of engineers. . . . Preparations for the overall operations must be completed by mid-August.
> 2. These preparations will include the creation of conditions which will make a landing in England possible:
>   a. The British air force must be so far neutralized . . . that it will offer no appreciable resistance to the German crossing operation;
>   b. Lanes must be cleared of mines;
>   c. Both outlets of the Straits of Dover, and the west entrance to the English Channel in a line approximately

from Alderney to Portland, must be sealed off by a dense belt of mines;

d. The coastal areas must be commanded and covered by the fire of heavy coastal artillery. . . .

The operation will be given the designation *Sea Lion*. During preparations and in the execution of the operation the missions of the three branches of the Wehrmacht will be as follows:

a. Army. Preparation of plans of operations and of a crossing plan initially for all units to be shipped in the first wave. . . .

b. Navy. Procurement and assembly of the required shipping space at the points of embarkation designated by the army and in accordance with nautical requirements. As far as possible use will be made of ships from defeated hostile countries. . . . Naval forces will protect the flanks of the entire movement across the channel.

c. Luftwaffe. The mission of the Luftwaffe will be to prevent interference by hostile air forces. In addition airpower will be employed to neutralize coastal fortifications which could deliver fire in the landing areas, to break the initial resistance offered by the hostile ground forces, and to destroy reserves during their forward movement. . . . It will also be important for air units to destroy roads which could be used by the enemy to move reserves forward, and to attack naval units approaching the areas of operations while still far distant from the crossing routes.

I request recommendations on the use of paratrooper and glider and other airborne forces. The question must be examined together with the army whether it would be wise to withhold paratrooper and other airborne forces during the initial stages as a reserve force which could be moved quickly to critical areas in the event of an emergency.*

---

* "Führer Directive 16," July 16, 1940, World War II Database. http://ww2db.com/doc.php?q=316.

(continued from page 39)

For France, however, the Dunkirk evacuation was the beginning of the end. After finishing off the rear guard on the English Channel coast, the Germans turned south and smashed the remainder of the French Army. On June 14, Paris fell. On June 22, Hitler received word from representatives of the French government that they wished to discuss peace terms. The German leader insisted that the document of surrender be signed in the same place, using the same railway carriage, in which the Germans had signed the armistice ending World War I in 1918; he later had the whole site destroyed.

With the French capitulation, Hitler was in a conciliatory mood. He had no particular wish to conquer Great Britain itself and was prepared to leave the British alone so long as they agreed to end the war and accept Germany's mastery of mainland Europe. Given what had just happened at Dunkirk, it was a reasonable, even generous, peace proposal. Many of Churchill's closest colleagues pressured him to accept it.

Churchill, however, believed that any peace with Germany in such a situation of weakness would only delay defeat, not avoid it. If Germany were allowed to consolidate its gains in Western Europe under the guise of peace, it would only be a matter of time before it renewed the war against Britain. It was better, Churchill argued, to go down fighting than accept such a humiliating "peace." With some difficulty, he won over his colleagues. Britain brusquely rejected Hitler's proposal for a cease-fire.

So the war would go on. Hitler reluctantly began plans for "Operation Sea Lion," the invasion of southern England. In London, Churchill broadcast to his people: "The Battle of France is over. . . . The Battle of Britain is about to begin."[2]

The Adversaries Prepare

Despite the German Army's recent triumph, its commanders were not very enthusiastic about Operation Sea Lion. The army had fought a grueling campaign in France and needed time to rest and reequip before embarking on any fresh military expeditions. More to the point, it had no experience with amphibious warfare: no specialist training, no equipment such as landing craft, and no detailed knowledge of what to expect in England or what the condition of the British Army was after Dunkirk. Crossing rivers was one thing, but crossing large bodies of water—even comparatively narrow ones such as the 21-mile (33.8-km) English Channel—was quite another. The army's staff officers went ahead with their planning in a mood of gloom.

If anything, the German Navy, the Kriegsmarine, was even less keen on the invasion plan than the army. It would be the navy's responsibility to defend the invasion flotilla from attack by sea. The British Royal Navy was the largest surface force in the world; in the event of impending assault against the British Isles, the Admiralty would throw every warship it had against the invaders. Moreover, Germany had lost a number of important vessels during the Norwegian campaign. There was no time to replace them now. Admiral Erich Raeder, commander of the Kriegsmarine, made little secret of his scorn for the whole plan.

Hermann Göring, the leader of the Luftwaffe, also opposed Sea Lion, but for different reasons. He thought it was unnecessary. In his opinion, the German air force was more than capable of overcoming Britain by itself without a ground invasion. Air superiority over southern England was vital to the success or failure of any attack. If the Royal Air Force could be battered into submission, Churchill would have no choice but to accept peace terms. A victory secured purely from the air would flatter Göring's vanity. He leaped at the chance, therefore, to impress Hitler with the devastating power of his Luftwaffe.

THE LUFTWAFFE

On the eve of the Battle of Britain, the pilots of the Luftwaffe rightly considered themselves to be the most highly trained and experienced group of military aviators in the world. Many had seen active service during the Spanish Civil War (1936–1939) and more recently had flown numerous combat missions over Poland and France. Their casualties up to this point in the war had been relatively light. They entered their fight with the RAF with a well-earned confidence in their own abilities.

In terms of numbers and quality of aircraft, the Luftwaffe was an impressive force. Despite some losses sustained in the Battle of France, on June 30, 1940, the German air force still had operational more than 1,100 single-engine fighters, 350 twin-engine fighters, 1,300 medium bombers, and nearly 450 dive-bombers.[1] These were organized into five *Luftflotten*, or air fleets, of which three were immediately committed against

The Messerschmitt Bf 109, a German fighter plane that was employed during the Battle of Britain, is seen here.

Britain. Two, Luftflotten 2 and 3, were stationed in northern France, and a third, Luftflotte 5, in Norway. Each Luftflotte was a mixture of fighter and bomber aircraft.

Germany's principal single-seat fighter in 1940, the Messerschmitt Bf 109E, was among the most outstanding aircraft of World War II. Originally flown in 1935, it was one of the first fighters of any nation to feature all-metal construction, a closed canopy, and retractable landing gear. Its powerful liquid-cooled, fuel-injection V-12 Daimler Benz engine gave it a maximum level speed of 348 mph (560 kph) and a ferocious dive and climb rate, and its armament of two 20mm cannons and two machine guns made it a deadly opponent. Although tricky to fly, the Bf 109 was beloved by its pilots; its success can be gauged by the fact that, in various modified forms, almost 34,000 were built during the war. Germany's other main fighter, the Messerschmitt Bf 110, had two engines and a crew of two. A so-called heavy or destroyer fighter with a much longer range than the Bf 109, it was originally designed to escort bomber aircraft over their targets. Although it would prove to be a formidable night fighter later in the war, the Bf 110's sluggish maneuverability would be a dangerous weakness during the Battle of Britain.

Aside from the Junkers Ju 87 Stuka, the main bombers employed by the Luftwaffe during the Battle of Britain were the

HERMANN GÖRING (1893–1946)

Hermann Göring was a ruthless and tyrannical man who is reviled today as one of his country's greatest villains. The future commander of the German air force was born in Bavaria into a wealthy and highly respected family. His father, Heinrich, was a soldier by profession and had served as Germany's first governor of its colony in southwest Africa (today known as Namibia). Göring went to military school and became an officer cadet in 1912. When World War I broke out in 1914, he initially served in an infantry regiment in France before being removed from the front line because of rheumatism. While recovering in the hospital, a friend suggested that Göring transfer to Germany's fledgling air force. After finishing his pilot's training course, he was posted to a fighter squadron in 1915. He went on to shoot down 22 enemy aircraft, making him one of Germany's leading aces. At the end of World War I, Göring was commanding the elite squadron formerly led by the "Red Baron," Manfred von Richthofen, who had died earlier in the year.

Göring was left bewildered by Germany's defeat in 1918 and sought an explanation for the military failure. He found it through Adolf Hitler's charismatic National Socialist movement, which contended that German socialists, pacifists, and most of all Jews were responsible for the nation's failure. Göring joined the Nazis in 1922 and took part a year later

Dornier Do 17, the Heinkel He 111, and the Junkers Ju 88. All three shared some basic characteristics. They were relatively small and light twin-engine aircraft with maximum bomb loads of 2,000 to 6,000 pounds (907 to 2,722 kilograms). For defense, they relied on a small number of manually aimed

---

in the party's attempt to seize control of Munich by force. During the failed revolt, Göring was shot in the leg. While recuperating from his wound in Austria, Göring was given the powerful but highly addictive painkiller morphine. The drug began to warp his personality; already a vain and arrogant man, Göring now became even more delusional and untrustworthy, contemptuous of others and certain of his own genius. It was a combination of traits that would help him rise in the Nazi leadership but would prove disastrous when he was tested as a military commander in World War II.

With Hitler's successful takeover of the German state in 1933, Göring became one of the most powerful men in the nation. In addition to being president of the Nazi-led parliament and prime minister of the important region of Prussia, Göring was given charge of the new Luftwaffe. By the time war broke out again in 1939, Göring commanded the world's greatest force of fighter and bomber aircraft. Even his eventual defeat in the Battle of Britain a year later did not diminish Göring's rising star. He was named Hitler's deputy and successor and built up a massive fortune by looting the wealth and art treasures of Germany's conquered territories.

Göring surrendered to American troops in May 1945. While waiting for his trial on war crimes charges, he was weaned off of morphine. Göring was sentenced to death for his complicity in Nazi Germany's worst crimes against humanity. His last "victory" of sorts was to cheat the hangman by poisoning himself the night before his planned execution.

machine guns operated by crewmen from the glazed central cockpits at the front of each aircraft. These large "fishbowl" Plexiglas windshields were designed to afford the pilot and navigator/bombardier maximum visibility.

Despite its experienced crews and large fleets of modern combat aircraft, however, the Luftwaffe would labor under some significant disadvantages during the Battle of Britain. Its greatest liability was that it was about to be asked to fight a kind of campaign that it had never been designed or trained to wage. From its earliest days, the Luftwaffe had been conceived as a close air-support arm for the German Army, providing the advancing troops with precision bombing strikes to knock out key ground targets. This it had done with great success in Poland, Norway, and France. The campaign against Britain, however, would be quite different. Rather than supporting a ground advance from short range, the Luftwaffe would now be expected to attack large strategic targets such as airfields, radar stations, and factories at long range. To do this properly, it really needed a four-engine heavy bomber similar to the Boeing B-17 "Flying Fortress" that was being introduced to the U.S. Army Air Forces around the same time, a plane with a large bomb load and long endurance in the air. No such plane as yet existed in the German arsenal. Worse, even when flying from French bases on the English Channel coast, the Bf 109 had too short a range to escort the bombers deep into British airspace. If ordered to attack inland targets, they would have to conduct the most dangerous part of their missions alone.

THE ROYAL AIR FORCE

In 1940, the RAF was organized differently from the Luftwaffe. Whereas the Germans operated mixed groups of aircraft types in air fleets, the British leadership structure was divided according to plane function. So Bomber Command controlled all of the RAF's bombers and Coastal Command its maritime patrol aircraft. The defense of the United Kingdom's airspace was entrusted to RAF Fighter Command, led throughout the Battle of Britain by Air Chief Marshal Sir Hugh Dowding. Fighter Command was further subdivided into four groups, each responsible for a specific geographical area. 11 Group, commanded by Sir Keith Park, covered London and southeast England and would be at the center of the upcoming battle.

Until the mid-1930s, Fighter Command had received low priority in the RAF's spending decisions. The prevailing wisdom at the time was that in any future war, bomber aircraft would be too fast and well armed for single-seat fighters to stop them and so fighter defense was a waste of money. This was true so long as fighters were still the fragile wood-and-fabric biplanes that had been used in World War I. Around 1935, however, a new generation of fighters started to be introduced: powerful, streamlined, all-metal monoplanes with multiple forward-firing machine guns or cannons. These new fighters were more than a match for the bombers they would be pitted against. So Fighter Command rapidly rose to the top of the RAF's pecking order.

The British counterparts to the Messerschmitt Bf 109 were the Supermarine Spitfire and the Hawker Hurricane. The Spitfire is perhaps the single best-known fighter aircraft in the history of aerial warfare; its distinctive silhouette with its elegant tapered wings is still instantly recognizable to aviation fans. Designed by R.J. Mitchell, who died shortly after the first prototype was completed, the Spitfire was the fastest combat aircraft available to the RAF in 1940 thanks to its formidable Rolls-Royce Merlin engine, a variant of which would also power the American P-51 Mustang later in the war. The Hurricane, a much less glamorous aircraft, never achieved the fame of its stable mate, but it was the more important of the pair during the Battle of Britain, accounting for almost two-thirds of all Fighter Command's combat kills. It was a little slower than the Spitfire but easier to fly and more rugged and stable all around. Many Battle of Britain pilots preferred the Hurricane because it lacked the temperamental behavior of the Spitfire and could absorb far greater damage. At the outset of the battle, the RAF had a total of 754 of both types to take on the Luftwaffe's 1,100 Bf 109s.[2]

The differences between the Fighter Command aircraft and the Bf 109 were more of degree than of kind. The German plane

EVACUATION

At the outbreak of war, more than 800,000 children and 500,000 mothers with infants were evacuated from Britain's major cities to the countryside because of fears of air-raid attacks. Operation Pied-Piper, as it was known, was an enormous and highly successful undertaking, although the personal experiences of individual evacuees varied a lot. Some children thrived in their new homes and enjoyed the opportunity of living in a part of Britain they had never before known. Others, however, suffered neglect and abuse at the hands of their temporary guardians. When he was six years old, Ray Evans and his brother Frank were evacuated from the working-class slums of Liverpool to a farm in North Wales. Ray describes his initial impressions of his new home:

> It was an old steam train that slowly rattled its way to its destination, stopping at practically every station to pick up more evacuees, and occasionally for water. By the time we boarded, all the seats in the compartments had been taken, so we stood in the corridor the entire journey. The train was very crowded, making it difficult to move around. I didn't mind at first, as I had a good view of the countryside through the window. I was so taken up seeing the sheep and cows and horses in the fields. . . . Throughout the journey lots of children were crying or sick.

had a higher maximum speed and was better at climbing and diving, but it was less maneuverable and had a larger turning circle. It performed better at high altitude than either the Spitfire or the Hurricane but worse at lower altitudes. So which of the

> The train eventually made its way across the Welsh border into the town of Llanelli. It blew its whistle as it entered the station, slowed down, and came to a halt alongside the platform. It was about 11 P.M., and Liverpool seemed a million miles away. We were very tired and hungry, and not in a very cooperative state. The novelty of my first train journey had worn off many hours ago. We all spilled out onto the station platform where we were lined up for a head count. I could hear people shouting in some foreign language [Welsh], but I couldn't see them properly for the steam that was whirling everywhere. Then someone behind us shouted: "I hope we're not in bloody Germany." . . .
>
> The Evacuee Distribution Centre was the place where our "borrowed" parents were waiting to make their choices. As we entered the hall, we were each given a brown paper bag. Inside were two cheese sandwiches and a few biscuits. For a beverage we had a choice of a cup of tea or glass of lemonade. The allocation of children to their foster parents was like a cattle market. . . . "I'll have that one." . . . "I'll take that one." . . . "I don't want that one, I want a boy." . . . Mrs. Davis, our billeting officer, said that it was getting very late and we had to leave right away. We all said goodbye to each other and raced to the cars out in the rain. Frank and I just sat in silence as we were driven through the dark, empty streets to our new home and new mother.*
>
> ---
> * Ray Evans, *Before the Last All Clear*. Garden City, N.Y.: Morgan James, 2008.

In this 1940 photo, a British Hawker Hurricane of Fighter Command is on its way to engage German bombers on the south coast of England during the Battle of Britain.

two sides had the advantage in any given combat depended on the exact circumstances of the battle. Individual pilot skill mattered much more than the characteristics of the planes.

The British did, however, have two important advantages over the Germans. One was that they were using highly refined 100-octane fuel imported from the United States, a better quality gasoline than that available to the Luftwaffe. In a close dogfight, this gave the British engines a slight edge in performance. The other advantage was that the battle was taking place over the United Kingdom itself, close to the RAF's own airfields.

Neither the Spitfire nor the Hurricane had a much better range than the Bf 109, but they did not have to fly so far to reach the combat zone in the first place. The RAF's fighter pilots could rest assured that they had plenty of places to land in an emergency, whereas even the greatest Luftwaffe ace always had to keep one anxious eye on his fuel gauge during a mission.

RADAR AND THE "DOWDING SYSTEM"

The British had two first-class fighter aircraft in the shape of the Spitfire and the Hurricane in 1940, but the heart of their defense was not these combat planes themselves so much as the RAF's command and control system. Without a proper means of identifying and prioritizing targets, the British would have soon lost the Battle of Britain regardless of what kinds of aircraft they had. Most of the Luftwaffe's planes were flying from bases just across the English Channel and arrived over United Kingdom airspace after barely a few minutes' flying. If they could catch the RAF's pilots on the ground, the Spitfires and Hurricanes would be destroyed before they could even take off. Fighter Command could not afford to fly continuous patrols; this would wear out its aircraft and pilots too quickly, and in any case, if they were relying on randomly encountering Luftwaffe raiders, then much of the time they would be at a numerical disadvantage in combat. Defeating the Germans required a comprehensive early-warning system and a way of getting defending fighters just where they needed to be at exactly the right time in the right numbers.

Luckily for the British, they did have just this kind of integrated defense scheme in 1940, known as the "Dowding System" after its main architect, the leader of Fighter Command, Sir Hugh Dowding. It relied on a mixture of advanced technology and sophisticated intelligence gathering and dissemination. The RAF was fortunate that Britain's early-warning Radio Direction Finding (RDF) network had just come into operation at the outbreak of World War II. Known as "Chain Home," it was a ring of monitoring stations encircling the eastern and southern coast of the United Kingdom. RDF, which is better known today as radar, sent out beams of electromagnetic radio waves that would bounce off any solid object in the sky (such as an aircraft) and reflect back the object's "shadow" to the transmitting station. Because radar technology was still in its infancy in 1940, Chain Home was vulnerable to false alarms, especially ones caused by bad weather. The system, however, gave Fighter Command a crucial few minutes of warning when the Germans were preparing a major raid on southern England, for the Chain Home operators could watch the Luftwaffe's air fleets assembling in the skies over their French bases.

RDF was only part of the Dowding System, however. Its real heart was at RAF Bentley Priory, the headquarters of Fighter Command in north London. Here, a group of senior officers received continuous updates from the Chain Home network as well as individual observers who were stationed along the English coastline to watch for incoming German planes. In this way they could plot in real time all enemy activity over the United Kingdom, analyzing the Luftwaffe's strategy on any given day and identifying the most critical threats at that moment. Bentley Priory was in telephone contact with all of Fighter Command's Group headquarters. When attacks were identified, the group commanders could be notified and they could then order their RAF squadrons to "scramble" into action when—and only when—they were most needed. By allocating its limited resources in this very efficient way, Fighter Command could consistently punch above its weight, with its Spitfires and Hurricanes being deployed at the point of greatest threat for the minimum amount of flying time. In contrast with the Germans, who largely made up their day-to-day strategy as they went along, the British were working to a well-conceived plan and stuck to it. This was to make a huge difference to the ultimate outcome of the Battle of Britain.

Eagle Day

Thanks to the evacuation at Dunkirk, the bulk of the British soldiers who had been trapped in France when the Germans surrounded them in May 1940 had escaped to fight another day. Most, however, returned to England with just their rifles. They had left almost all of their heavy equipment—tanks, artillery pieces, trucks, and ammunition—behind. It would take months, perhaps years, to rebuild this shattered force to its former strength. In the meantime, the British Army could offer only very limited resistance to any would-be invader.

In desperation, Churchill's government appealed to all men too young or too old for service as regular soldiers to join an emergency militia. The response was terrific; by the beginning of July 1940, 1.5 million Britons had volunteered. This force, originally called the Local Defence Volunteers (LDV) and later the Home Guard, possessed tremendous enthusiasm and bravery but lacked any modern training or equipment. Apart from a few World War I-era rifles, there were no weapons to spare at first; the volunteers were left to procure them as best they could, and so attics and museum cases were raided for rusty shotguns and muskets. Some men relied on nothing more than pikes and kitchen knives tied to broomsticks. While the Home Guard was an inspired morale boost to the British, it seemed unlikely that it would trouble any German invaders if the troops of Operation Sea Lion managed to get a successful foothold on the English shore.

To many observers, Britain's chances of surviving the summer seemed bleak. Joseph P. Kennedy, the father of a future U.S. president, John F. Kennedy, was President Franklin Roosevelt's ambassador in London at the time. Kennedy was convinced that the British would collapse in a matter of weeks and argued that the United States, which was still neutral, should not waste any of its resources helping Churchill's government. Some observers were even blunter about Britain's chances. General Maxime Weygand, who had commanded the French Army in the days immediately before its defeat, was scornful: "England will have her neck wrung like a chicken."[1]

Before any German invasion attempt could be mounted, the Luftwaffe had to secure command of the air over the beaches of Kent and Sussex. It was in order to secure this crucial preliminary step that Göring and his commanders drew up their plans in July 1940. The Luftwaffe leader spelled out his instructions in simple terms: "[U]ntil the enemy air force has been broken, the overriding principle behind air operations is to attack the enemy's flying units at every favorable opportunity, by day and by night, on the ground and in the air, without regard to any other tasks."[2]

THE CHANNEL BATTLES

The Luftwaffe's initial idea was to launch fighter sweeps across southern England, hoping to draw out 11 Group's Spitfires and

Hurricanes and whittle their numbers down in single combat. Hugh Dowding, however, was too vigilant to allow his squadrons to be depleted by such an obvious ploy. During the Battle of France, he had suffered Churchill's wrath by adamantly refusing to release more fighters to assist the French. The absence of the RAF over the skies of Dunkirk had allowed the Germans to wreak great damage on the evacuating army, but Dowding's caution had paid off in the long run: Fighter Command's strength had been preserved. Now he had no intention of squandering his aircraft in diversionary skirmishes.

Göring's men realized that they would have to find an alternative kind of target, something the RAF would have to defend. They settled on the English channel convoys. Despite the French coast being in enemy hands, the British were still sending merchant ships through the channel to and from the port of London. These slow-moving, lightly armed vessels were vulnerable to attack from the air. For the Luftwaffe, raids on these convoys would force the British into combat and also provide the German aircrews with valuable experience for the ultimate clash still to come.

The first of these attacks, as previously mentioned, came on July 10, 1940. Many more were to follow during the next four weeks. The channel battles were quite costly for the RAF. More than 160 of its fighters were destroyed, plus about the same number damaged—about a fifth of Fighter Command's entire strength. At such a rate of loss, the RAF would eventually cease to exist. For all these efforts, the RAF was unable to defend merchant ships traveling through the channel. Convoys had to be canceled to prevent further losses. Dover, which was close enough to France to be shelled by long-range artillery, experienced constant harassment attacks by German raiders and became known as "Hellfire Corner."

Still, it was not all bad news for the British. One early discovery was that the Messerschmitt Bf 110 was quite unable to

(continues on page 60)

SIR HUGH DOWDING (1882–1970)

The operational leaders of the opposing air forces in the Battle of Britain were polar opposites. Whereas the Luftwaffe's Hermann Göring was a swollen giant of a man, vain and egotistical, though not without charm, Air Chief Marshal Sir Hugh Dowding, commanding officer of RAF Fighter Command, came across as reedy, mouselike, and emotionally distant. Yet while Dowding may have cut a meek figure, the crisis of 1940 showed his true mettle. His unruffled calm in the midst of the emergency and his prudent, intelligent handling of the RAF's limited resources probably saved Britain from invasion.

Dowding was born in the Scottish town of Moffat and later educated at Winchester, an elite private school in England. In 1899, he joined the British Army as an artillery officer. While in the army, he became interested in the fledgling world of aviation, earning his pilot's license shortly before the outbreak of World War I. At the war's start, he transferred to the Royal Flying Corps, the precursor to the RAF, and served as a fighter pilot, eventually becoming a squadron commander. He remained in the air force at the end of hostilities and rose steadily up the ranks, learning in the process much about training, supply, and organization. Personal tragedy struck Dowding when his wife died suddenly, and he was left to take care of their infant son alone. Traumatized, he devoted himself to his work, developing in the process a reputation for being dull and humorless.

In 1936, Dowding was placed in charge of RAF Fighter Command, just at the fateful moment when fast monoplane fighters such as the Spitfire and Hurricane were com-

Air Chief Marshal Hugh Dowding was the commander of RAF Fighter Command during the Battle of Britain and is widely credited with bringing victory to the British during this crucial battle.

ing into service and radar was in development. Dowding's genius was to tie these technologies together into an integrated defense system for the whole United Kingdom. The "Dowding System" was instrumental to the RAF's eventual victory in 1940.

At the outbreak of World War II, Dowding was nearing retirement age, but he was asked to stay on at Fighter Command until a suitable replacement could be found. Thus by chance he was still in charge of Britain's main line of defense in the crisis year of 1940. His prickly temper did not win him many friends and he alienated some of his subordinate officers, such as 12 Group Commander Trafford Leigh-Mallory, who schemed to have Dowding removed as

(continues)

(continued)
soon as possible. In November 1940, the month following the official end of the Battle of Britain, Dowding was replaced. The circumstances of his departure from Fighter Command, so soon after its greatest victory, remain controversial to this day.

Dowding spent his retirement researching and writing about spiritualism and supernatural forces. He had always had unusual religious beliefs, rejecting Christianity and believing fervently in reincarnation and the existence of ghosts and fairies. His beliefs, together with the lingering public row about whether Dowding had been unfairly treated in 1940, discouraged the postwar RAF from giving him the honorary post of Marshal of the Royal Air Force, the highest honor it could bestow.

(continued from page 57)
combat Hurricanes and Spitfires on equal terms. Göring had taken great pride in these heavy fighters, but they were simply too cumbersome to survive in a dogfight. The Luftwaffe leader's own nephew was killed flying in a Bf 110 in the first few days of the English Channel battle. Now that the Bf 110's vulnerability had been exposed, Bf 109s had to be delegated to protect the twin-engine planes, diluting the total German attack strength.

ATTACK ON RADAR STATIONS

The attacks on channel convoys were intended merely as a preliminary to the main aerial confrontation. By the third week of August 1940, the Luftwaffe was ready to take the battle to its next stage. August 13 was chosen as "Eagle Day"—*Adlertag*—marking the commencement of the direct assault on the British mainland. First, however, it would be necessary to knock out the RAF's early-warning system. So on August 12, a large German force of fighters and bombers was dispatched to attack the Radio Direction Finding stations scattered along the Kent and East Sussex coast at Dover, Pevensey, and Rye.

The Luftwaffe pressed home its attacks with ferocity. Within a few hours, all three RDF stations were out of action. A great hole had been torn in the Chain Home "curtain" protecting the British coastline. Once the smoke had cleared and the radar operators had emerged from their bomb shelters, however, it took surprisingly little time to restore the stations to operation. Their tall radio masts were difficult to destroy, and much of the damage turned out to be easily reparable. The RDF personnel, most of whom were women serving in the Women's Auxiliary Air Force (WAAF), continued throughout the battle to work long hours, under great pressure and the constant threat of attack, patching any gaps that had formed in Chain Home.

Had the Luftwaffe concentrated the weight of its bombing on the RDF stations throughout the remainder of August, even the best efforts of the WAAF might not have been enough to keep Britain's crucial radar screen operational. Yet strangely, after August 12, the Germans never properly followed up their initial attacks. They seem to have erroneously assumed that they had put the southeastern RDF stations permanently out of commission. They also did not seem to have fully understood the enormous value of radar to the RAF as part of the Dowding System. Had they done so, the story of the Battle of Britain might have turned out very differently. It was a critical failure of imagination on the part of the Luftwaffe.

The attacks on the RDF stations revealed another unwelcome truth to the Germans. Their Junkers Ju 87 Stuka dive-bombers, which had wreaked so much havoc above Poland and France, had always flown in skies dominated by their own fighters. Now, for the first time, they were being sent into airspace not controlled by the Luftwaffe. The results were

(continues on page 64)

RADAR

What the British in the 1930s called "Radio Direction Finding" is today much better known as *radar* (a short form of "Radio and Detection Ranging"). In this short account, Michael Pollick explains how radar works:

> If you've ever shouted at a distant building or hillside and heard an echo, you've experienced the basic principle behind radar. Sound-waves from your mouth move through the air at approximately 600 mph (966 kph). If there is nothing substantial in front of you, these sound-waves travel a certain distance and dissipate. But if those sound-waves strike the side of a building or the surface of a lake or a cliff wall, a portion of them are reflected back to the source. Your ears pick up the words you shouted a few seconds earlier. If you have a very sensitive stopwatch and good hearing, you can clock the time between your shouted words and the instant you hear the echo. This is essentially what radar does. . . .
>
> In order to understand the more complicated principles of radar, it is useful to examine each element by itself:
>
> 1. *Radio.* A radio transmitter is used to send out a series of electronic pulses into the air. This transmitter is often mounted on a rotating device in order to sweep the entire area around the radar tower. Instead of moving at the speed of sound, these pulses move at nearly the speed of light. Once a pulse is sent out, it is tracked by a receiver system. If the pulse is not blocked by an object, it will continue outward until it dissipates. Consequently, the receiver will not pick up a return signal and the radar screen will remain blank in that particular area. But if the pulse strikes an object, some of the wave will be reflected back to the tower. . . . The radar screen will contain a visible

dot at this location. Once all of the individual pulses have been received and measured, the entire screen will show where all the signals were reflected. A trained operator can then use this information to determine what objects were encountered.

2. *Detection.* The first thing a basic radar system can do is detect a solid object in the area it scans sonically. The transmitter sends out a pulse of radio waves and eventually they strike an object. By measuring the time it takes to send out the signal and receive its echo, a radar operator can calculate the distance of the object from the radar array. Since radio waves move so fast, this time is often measured in microseconds. If a solid object continues to be picked up in the same place, the radar operator can assume the object is not moving. . . .

3. *Ranging.* A pulse of radio waves can detect a solid object simply by measuring reflectivity towards the tower, but this reading alone does not indicate movement. In order to estimate the range and movement of an object, more sophisticated readings must be taken. The basic principle behind these readings is called a *Doppler shift*. One common example of Doppler shift occurs when a police car approaches from a distance and the tone of the siren seems to become higher. This apparent change in pitch is caused by a Doppler shift. The siren's true pitch and volume never changed from the moment it was activated, but the listener receives a higher concentration of sound-waves as the car grew closer. The tone changed because the frequency of these concentrated waves became higher. As the car moves away, the siren's sound-waves slow down and the tone is lower. In order to calculate an object's speed on radar, the system must take this Doppler shift into account.*

---

* Source: "Electronic Devices: How Radar Works," Essortment.com. "http://www.essortment.com/hobbies/electronicdevic_sfbq.htm.

(continued from page 61)

embarrassing and deadly. However terrifying the Stuka might seem to someone on the ground, to the waiting Spitfires and Hurricanes the dive-bomber was easy prey. It was far too slow to avoid the British hunters and its armament of a single machine gun fired from the rear was virtually useless as a defense. Stukas were shot down in droves. Soon the Luftwaffe had to quietly withdraw the beleaguered Ju 87 squadrons from the battle before they were all lost to the RAF's guns.

THE BATTLE FOR THE AIRFIELDS BEGINS

Göring was undeterred by the German losses. Adlertag, he was convinced, would see the beginning of the end for Fighter Command. On August 13, the entire force of Luftflotten 2 and 3 would be thrown at 11 Group's airfields in Kent. If these could be knocked out of action, this crucial sector of the RAF's defenses would be neutralized, forcing the British to withdraw farther inland and leaving the invasion beaches not properly protected.

Because there was heavy rain across Kent on August 13, the main German attack had to be recalled. The attackers returned the following day, however, and the tempo of the battle increased until its climax on August 18, after which there was a temporary respite because of exhaustion on both sides and the return of bad weather. August 18 would become known as "The Hardest Day" of the entire Battle of Britain, as it saw the greatest casualties for both the RAF and the Luftwaffe. In that 24-hour period, the British lost 34 Hurricanes and Spitfires in the air and another 29 were blown up on the ground before they could take off, while the Germans suffered the destruction of 69 fighters and bombers. Many of the main bases of 11 Group, including RAF Biggin Hill, RAF Kenley, and RAF Manston, were so battered by German bombs that they had to be closed for repairs, with their fighters scattered to emergency satellite airstrips.

The British were discovering dangerous weaknesses in their tactical preparation. The standard formation for fighters officially authorized by the RAF was made up of three aircraft flown tightly together and was called a "Vic." It was a rigid, inflexible arrangement that allowed individual pilots little scope for using their initiative and left the whole formation vulnerable to attack. RAF senior commanders, however, insisted on using it even after its limitations had been revealed in combat. By contrast, the Luftwaffe flew its fighters in pairs, one pilot the leader and the other his wingman, with two pairs making up a loose combination called a "swarm" (*Schwarm*). This arrangement was far more effective in close combat, so much so that the leader-wingman pairing remains the basis of fighter tactics even today. Ultimately, the RAF would adopt it too, but not before many Spitfire and Hurricane pilots were unnecessarily lost.

It may not seem surprising that the Germans were feeling highly pleased with themselves by August 18. In the wake of Adlertag, they had neutralized many of the RAF's forward airfields and shot down significant numbers of its fighters. Much of this confidence was, however, based on a wild overestimation of the number of British aircraft they had eliminated. After the confusion of combat, it was often very hard to verify all the "kills" claimed by one's own side. Several fighter pilots had often fired at the same enemy plane, each assuming afterward that he had shot down a different aircraft. The fate of damaged fighters and bombers was often unclear: Those that did not immediately crash slipped away from the combat area, some to crash-land or ditch in the sea and others to limp back to their bases.

Figuring out what exactly had happened at the end of the day was, then, quite an intelligence problem. The British had an advantage in that many German planes had crashed in southern England and could be directly accounted for. Also, they debriefed their returning pilots more critically than the Luftwaffe did, and overall took a more sober, realistic view of the kills they had inflicted. The result was that while both sides overestimated to some degree the losses the enemy had received, the German figures were far more inflated. Overall, the Luftwaffe exaggerated its combat kills by a factor of three. Little wonder then that by the final week of August 1940, its pilots had convinced themselves that the RAF was crumbling and that just a little more ramping up of the pressure would break Britain's defensive wall for good.

The RAF at Bay

After a break of a few days because of poor weather, the Battle of Britain resumed on August 24, 1940. For the next two weeks, each day unfolded much like the previous one. The Germans would send multiple attacking waves of bombers escorted by Bf 109s to harass the RAF's forward airfields in Kent and East Sussex. Fighter Command would scramble its defending Spitfires and Hurricanes and a series of escalating dogfights would ensue over the skies of southeastern England.

Although neither side had gained any decisive advantage, conditions in 11 Group were looking grim by the end of August. Six out of the seven major airfields in that sector were out of action because of bomb damage, which meant that 11 Group's fighters had to operate from scattered emergency airstrips. This made it harder to coordinate their attacks on the Luftwaffe. More dangerous still, RAF pilots were being lost at a much faster rate than they could be replaced. Those who had survived the battle so far were exhausted. Worn down by constant flying and lack of sleep, they were starting to make mistakes in combat through fatigue, mistakes that could often prove fatal. Hugh Dowding had no choice but to rotate his veteran pilots in 11 Group to stations farther inland for temporary rest and recuperation. While this allowed them to regain their strength, it meant that their place in the front line had to be taken up by novice pilots who stood little chance against the aces of the Luftwaffe.

In public, Winston Churchill, Dowding, and the other British leaders put on a brave face. In private, they were gloomy and anxious. The RAF seemed to be losing the Battle of Britain. Operation Sea Lion loomed ever more ominously on the horizon.

ARGUMENTS ABOUT TACTICS

Perhaps given the intense stress that all the senior commanders were under at this point, it is not surprising that arguments broke out about how best to use the RAF's remaining resources. In particular, there was a running battle of words between 11 Group's Sir Keith Park and the leader of 12 Group, Sir Trafford Leigh-Mallory.

While Park's 11 Group was at the very heart of the battle in southeastern England, Leigh-Mallory's 12 Group was located farther north, defending East Anglia and the Midlands. Leigh-Mallory was a firm advocate of what became known as the "Big Wing." The idea was that rather than throwing individual squadrons of Spitfires and Hurricanes at the attacking Germans as soon as they became available, it was best to assemble a large formation of fighter squadrons and strike the German attack groups en masse. Leigh-Mallory's faith in the Big Wing was backed up by one of his most famous squadron leaders, the double-amputee Douglas Bader. Together, the pair demanded that Dowding let them pursue their tactical plan.

Park was outraged. He reminded Leigh-Mallory that 12 Group's main job was to defend 11 Group's airfields while Park's own fighters were off intercepting the German attack wave. The problem with the Big Wing was that it took time to assemble in the sky. While the 12 Group fighters were busy getting into formation, Park's airfields were left without their protective aerial cover. The result was that by the time the Big Wing was ready to pounce, the Luftwaffe had already swooped in, leaving a trail of destruction. Since Leigh-Mallory's own airfields were rarely attacked, he did not seem to be aware of the tremendous pressure this was putting on 11 Group. Leigh-Mallory was unrepentant, insisting that Big Wings were the only really effective way to destroy large numbers of German raiders.

The argument raged throughout the summer and autumn of 1940. Both sides had a point. When a Big Wing got itself into the right position at the right time, its effect could be devastating, as the events of September 15 would show. More often than not, however, it was a disappointment. Dowding tried, not very successfully, to act as a neutral referee between his feuding commanders, but Leigh-Mallory and Bader became convinced that the Fighter Command chief was deliberately thwarting their plans and began plotting to have him removed. The decision to effectively sack Dowding shortly after the end of the Battle of Britain probably had a lot to do with the bad feeling created by the Big Wing dispute.

On the other side of the English Channel, the Germans were having arguments of their own. The German successes against Fighter Command were being won at a heavy cost, especially to the Luftwaffe's bomber crews. The Do 17s, He 111s, and Ju 88s were proving to be highly vulnerable to machine-gun attack. The bomber commanders complained to Hermann Göring that the German fighters were not providing a sufficiently tight escort. To placate his men, Göring told the

(continues on page 72)

DOUGLAS BADER (1910–1982)

After a devastating air crash at age 21 caused the amputation of both of his legs, Douglas Bader defied his doctors' predictions that he could never lead a normal life. He first learned to walk on artificial legs without the aid of a stick, then retrained himself to fly, and finally returned to the Royal Air Force as a squadron leader during the Battle of Britain. Bader became one of the RAF's top-scoring aces during World War II, shooting down at least 20 German opponents. During the postwar era, the image of the legendary Bader with his stiff telltale gait became permanently associated with the defiance and stubborn resistance of 1940.

Bader's father was an officer in the Royal Engineers who died from injuries received in World War I when the boy was 12. After his mother remarried, she paid little attention to her son, and Bader grew up to be a highly competitive but unruly child. He excelled at sports, and this helped him to win a coveted scholarship to attend RAF Cranwell as an officer cadet. Following graduation in 1930, he joined a RAF squadron as a fighter pilot. The following year, while in training for the annual air show at Hendon, he was dared by another pilot to attempt a dangerous low-level loop. His aircraft crashed, and Bader, barely alive, was rushed to a hospital where his legs were amputated. He spent the next two years slowly learning to walk again on a pair of artificial legs.

Bader spent the remainder of the 1930s rebuilding his life. He got an office job, taught himself to play golf, and drove a specially modified car. But with the outbreak of war, he yearned to fly for the RAF again. After endless pestering, Bader was permitted to take an evaluation test and passed with flying colors. He was posted to a Spitfire squad-

Although left legless after a plane crash, Douglas Bader learned to fly again with artificial legs and fought in the Battle of Britain. One of the RAF's most successful pilots, he was shot down in France in August 1941 and spent the remainder of the war as a prisoner. He was knighted in 1976.

ron in January 1940, later switching to Hurricanes and then back to Spitfires. Bader was promoted to command a squadron in Trafford Leigh-Mallory's 12 Group and became a close ally and confidant of his leader, the two of them urging the use of "Big Wings" despite the resistance of 11 Group commander Sir Keith Park. Bader became a top-scoring pilot in his own right. Ironically, his disability gave him an edge in combat over men with normal legs. With his much shorter frame, he did not experience the same degree of dizziness when pulling tight turns caused by the dispersion of blood from the head to the feet.

After the Battle of Britain, Bader led a number of fighter-sweeps over German-occupied France. During one of these in August 1941, his plane was shot down and he was taken into captivity. Bader lost one of his artificial legs in the crash and such was the Germans' respect for their prisoner that they permitted the RAF to fly over a replacement. He repeatedly but unsuccessfully attempted to escape from prison camp and ended the war incarcerated in the famous Colditz castle. In his later life, Bader became a spokesman for disability charities and was knighted in 1976.

(continued from page 69)
fighter squadrons that henceforth they would have to stick even closer than before to the bombers.

To the Bf 109 pilots, this was ridiculous. The fighter was a hunter (*Jäger*); its key strength lay in its ability to pounce with great swiftness from above. If Bf 109s were required to fly right alongside the bomber stream, weaving constantly back and forth so as to keep at the same pace as the slower Do 17s, He 111s, and Ju 88s, then they would abandon the critical advantages of surprise and speed. Even though Göring himself was a former fighter pilot, he ignored these complaints, accusing his subordinates of lacking courage. The result was that the magnificent Schwarm tactics of the Luftwaffe fighters were squandered in a vain attempt to defend the bombers.

THE PILOTS

During the summer of 1940, one witness to the Battle of Britain, Virginia Cowles, wrote "You knew the fate of civilization was being decided fifteen thousand feet above your head in a world of sun, wind, and sky." What astonished Cowles most of all was that the future of the world lay in the hands of "little boys with blonde hair and pink cheeks who looked as though they ought to be in school."[1] The pilots on both sides seemed ridiculously young to have such responsibility foisted on their shoulders. Dog fighting, however, was a physically grueling job. It required good eyesight, intense concentration, and the ability to endure long and uncomfortable hours in a cockpit without losing focus. Dowding insisted that none of his squadron leaders be older than 26, as he believed older men could not take the strain of continual aerial combat. During the Battle of Britain, then, both sides placed their trust in a gaggle of young men who in normal circumstances might have been starting college or holding junior positions in office jobs.

To those without prewar flying experience, little preparation was available. At the height of the battle, British training

The RAF at Bay

RAF fighter pilots run for their planes. Despite the great pressures placed on each man, RAF pilots remained professional throughout the Battle of Britain and demonstrated considerable skill, resolve, and fortitude for months on end.

units were churning out novice pilots at a furious rate but with dangerously little flying time. Corners had to be cut in the training program; the rookies arrived at their operational squadrons with barely a few hours of practical experience in Spitfires or Hurricanes. The real training ground was the sky, where new pilots either learned their skills rapidly or suffered a quick demise at the hands of some Luftwaffe veteran. The Germans came into the battle with much more combat experience, but they were not rotated in and out of the front line for rest as the British pilots were. So, by the end of August, even the steeliest of Bf 109 aces was starting to feel the strain. Some men were so tired that they fell asleep in their cockpits immediately upon landing.

PLASTIC SURGERY

Richard Hillary (1919-1943) was an Australian-born RAF pilot who flew Spitfires throughout the Battle of Britain. On September 3, 1940, his aircraft was ambushed by a Bf 109 and caught fire. Hillary was able to bail out and parachuted into the North Sea, where he was rescued by a motor-launch, but he had been badly burned in the face and hands. At Queen Victoria Hospital in Sussex, he became a member of Sir Archibald McIndoe's celebrated "Guinea Pig Club," men who were undergoing experimental plastic surgery to reconstruct their damaged bodies following harrowing burns. Hillary described his first memories following the crash in his 1942 memoir:

> I was falling. Falling slowly through a dark pit. I was dead. My body, headless, circled in front of me. I saw it with my mind, my mind that was the redness in front of the eye, the dull scream in the ear, the grinning of the mouth, the ski crawling on the skull. It was death and resurrection. Terror, moving with me, touched my cheek with hers and I felt the flesh wince. Faster, faster. . . . I was hot now, hot, again with the body, on fire and screaming soundlessly. Dear God, no! No! Not that, not again. The sickly smell of death was in my nostrils and a confused roar of sound. Then it was all quiet. I was back.
> Someone was holding my arms.
> "Quiet now. There's a good boy. You're going to be all right. You've been very ill and you mustn't talk."

Flying a World War II-era combat aircraft was inherently dangerous—even leaving aside the small matter of the enemy trying to kill you. Fighter aircraft were built for performance and

> I tried to reach up my hand but could not.
> "Is that you, nurse? What have they done to me?"
> "Well, they've put something on your face and hands to stop them hurting and you won't be able to see for a little while. But you mustn't talk; you're not strong enough yet."
> Gradually I realized what had happened. My face and hands had been scrubbed and then sprayed with tannic acid. The acid had formed into a hard black cement. My eyes alone had received different treatment: they were coated with a thick layer of gentian violet. My arms were propped up in front of me, the fingers extended like witch's claws, and my body was hung loosely on straps just clear of the bed.
> I can recollect no moments of acute agony in the four days which I spent in that hospital. . . . Every three hours I was injected with morphia, so while imagining myself quite coherent I was for the most part in a semi-stupor. The memory of it has remained a confused blur. . . .
> [My parents] arrived in the afternoon and were met by Matron. Outside my ward a twittery nurse explained that they must not expect to find me looking quite normal, and they were ushered in. . . . For the sake of decorum my face had been covered with white gauze, with a slit in the middle through which protruded my lips.*
>
> **After extensive surgery, Hillary eventually returned to active service in the RAF. He was killed in January 1943 when his bomber aircraft crashed during a night training flight.**
>
> ---
> * Richard Hillary, *The Last Enemy*. London: Macmillan, 1942.

firepower, not safety. Accidents were common and often fatal. The greatest fear was not of machine gun bullets or cannon shells but of fire. Pilots were literally sitting on large tanks full of highly flammable aviation fuel. If a fire broke out in the cockpit, a pilot had about nine seconds to bail out before being overwhelmed by the smoke and flames. Even those who survived suffered horrific burns. The medical art of plastic surgery was pioneered during the war by New Zealand surgeon Archibald McIndoe, who did wonders rebuilding the badly disfigured faces and bodies of RAF pilots whose planes had caught fire in combat.

Despite the prospect of death, the pilots on both sides remained remarkably cool-headed about their job. There was little hatred. Luftwaffe fighter pilots considered themselves an elite class of warrior knights and spoke of their British counterparts with the professional respect due to skilled adversaries. The RAF men admired the Germans' courage, though they were nevertheless determined to chase these uninvited trespassers out of British skies. Both sides had a culture of "eat, drink, and be merry," knowing that the day to come could be their last on Earth. It was a strange sort of life: one minute carousing happily with fellow pilots, dining in fine restaurants, and flirting with girls; the next, strapped into a tiny cockpit at 15,000 feet (4,572 m) with only a thin screen of Perspex between them and the enemy's machine-gun fire.

HITLER LOSES PATIENCE

By the first week of September 1940, German intelligence reports indicated that so many British fighters had been destroyed that the RAF must be on the verge of disintegration. Yet frustratingly, each day their bombers were met by new waves of Spitfires and Hurricanes. A change in strategy was in order.

Up to this point, the German attacks had been concentrated mostly on military targets alone: airfields, radar stations, and other RAF facilities. Only very limited attempts had been made to knock out economic targets, such as aircraft factories, docks, or power plants. In part, this was due to Hitler's insistence that British civilian casualties be avoided, especially in London. Hitler, however, was not moved by humanitarian concerns. (He had been quite happy for the Luftwaffe to bomb defenseless civilians in Poland and France earlier in the war.) He was concerned that attacks on British civilians would provoke RAF Bomber Command to launch retaliatory raids on German cities. Additionally, because he hoped that the British could be persuaded to discuss peace terms without the need for an invasion, he worried that bombing London or Britain's other big cities would only stiffen his enemy's determination to continue fighting.

A series of accidents, however, caused Hitler to reconsider his earlier caution. On the night of August 23, a Luftwaffe bombing raid missed its target and dropped bombs on the suburb of Harrow, on the outskirts of London. The RAF responded by launching a raid of its own on Berlin. Neither of these raids caused significant damage or loss of life, but both Hitler and Göring were furious that the German capital had been attacked. The Luftwaffe commander had always insisted that his air force would prevent an attack on Berlin; he was personally humiliated by the RAF's actions. In a speech given on September 4, Hitler ranted: "If [the British] declare that they will attack our cities on a large scale, we will erase theirs! We will put a stop to the game of these night-pirates. . . . The hour will come when one or the other of us will crumble, and that one will not be National Socialist Germany."[2]

Some historians have exaggerated the significance of the tit-for-tat raids that started on August 23. It was likely Hitler and Göring were leaning toward attacking London anyway. The RAF's bombing of Berlin, however, gave the Germans the perfect excuse to abandon their earlier restraint. Feigning outrage, they now determined to reduce the British capital to rubble. Unbeknownst to them at the time, it would be the turning point of the Battle of Britain.

The Blitz

Saturday, September 7, 1940, was an uncharacteristically hot and beautiful day for England in early fall. By afternoon, temperatures had reached 90 degrees Fahrenheit (32 degrees Celsius). In the filter room at RAF Bentley Priory, headquarters of Fighter Command, the controllers waited for the day's "trade" from the Luftwaffe. Sure enough, around four o'clock in the afternoon a huge formation of enemy aircraft could be observed on radar forming up across the English Channel. Soon, a fleet of 348 Luftwaffe bombers and 617 escorting Bf 109s and Bf 110s—the largest concentration of German planes yet seen over British airspace—began moving slowly northwest toward Kent. The aerial armada formed a block 20 miles (32.2 km) wide, filling 800 square miles (1,287.5 square kilometers) of sky; the whole of southern England seemed overcast by the square black crosses of Dorniers, Heinkels, and Junkers.

At Bentley Priory, the controllers tried to anticipate when the throng of planes would split up to attack 11 Group's airfields. Yet strangely, it stayed together as a single massive body. The usual targets of Biggin Hill, Kenley, and Manston were ignored. The Germans moved inexorably toward the River Thames estuary. Eventually, as they grew closer to the outskirts of London, their target finally became obvious. Air-raid sirens wailed across the British capital as Londoners headed to their bomb shelters, many of them no doubt thinking that it was just another false alarm as so many others had been that summer. London, after all, had been largely spared the Luftwaffe's attentions so far.

Olive McNeil, who in 1940 was 14 and lived with her parents and two little brothers in the London borough of Poplar, later recalled what happened next:

> I could hear this strange droning sound. Looking up I could see lots of planes very small and very high. I called the boys to look. We said how pretty they looked with the sun glinting on them. They looked like stars. . . . Suddenly everything changed. The planes that were high up started to swoop down and the air was filled with screaming whistling sounds. The siren was blowing and mum came running out and pushed us down the shelter. We all screamed.[1]

LONDON IN FLAMES

It was the East End of London with its dockyards, warehouses, and tightly packed working-class tenement houses that suffered the worst of the blow on "Black Saturday." The German planes carried a mixture of high explosive and incendiary bombs. First the high explosives would blow the roofs off of buildings. Then the incendiaries, slim and sinister-looking canisters made of thermite, would lodge themselves in nooks and crannies of the rubble. Once ignited, thermite would set anything it touched instantly on fire, burning so hot it could bore through solid steel. The Germans knew that London's docklands contained large quantities of flammable materials; they would provide the perfect powder keg for the bombs.

EDWARD R. MURROW (1908–1965)

"*This . . .* is London." With this signature catchphrase, Edward R. Murrow began his nightly radio broadcasts to the people of America during the height of the Blitz on the British capital. Murrow brought the war in Europe into millions of American homes, portraying the battle of ordinary Londoners against the Nazi bombers as a conflict between democracy and despotism. It was partly thanks to Murrow's broadcasts that public sympathy in the still-neutral United States swung sharply toward Britain, allowing President Franklin D. Roosevelt's administration to provide more aid and assistance to the United Kingdom in its hour of greatest need.

Murrow had been born in Greensboro, North Carolina, in a small log cabin with neither electricity nor plumbing. When he was 6, the family moved to Washington state, where he later attended high school and college. In 1932, Murrow took a job at the Institute of International Education in New York, where he helped refugee Jewish scholars who had fled Germany because of the rise of Nazism. In 1935, he became a journalist, working for the Columbia Broadcasting System (CBS), the company that would employ him for the rest of his career. CBS sent Murrow to London to be its chief European correspondent.

His big break came in March 1938, when Hitler annexed Austria. The CBS team put together a special news report

By evening, the Surrey Commercial Dock, in which 1.5 million tons (1.36 billion kg) of wood were being stored, was burning so fiercely that the chief fire officer signaled despairingly to

---

on the fast-changing events, with Murrow reporting live from the Austrian capital, Vienna. Although this kind of on-the-spot journalism is commonplace today, it had never been attempted before until Murrow and his team tried it. With the outbreak of war in 1939, Murrow continued to make live broadcasts from London. During the Blitz, Murrow reported from the rooftop of the British Broadcasting Corporation (BBC) headquarters, watching the bombs fall around him and describing the sea of fire below. He made no secret of his sympathy for Britain's war effort and cast the Battle of Britain in stark terms as one of freedom versus tyranny. Murrow's influence back in the United States was considerable. When he returned to America shortly before the Japanese attack on Pearl Harbor in December 1941, Roosevelt honored him for having woken ordinary Americans out of their isolationist slumbers.

Murrow continued to broadcast for CBS as a war correspondent, reporting directly from bombing missions over Germany, until the end of the war. In one of his most famous programs in April 1945, he described in simple and devastating language the liberation of the concentration camp at Buchenwald. After the war, Murrow, now the most famous and respected journalist in the United States, moved into the new medium of television. In the early 1950s, he was one of the few public figures in America willing to openly criticize the excesses of Senator Joseph McCarthy's anticommunist "Red Scare." Shortly before his death, Britain's Queen Elizabeth II awarded Murrow an honorary knighthood for his wartime assistance to her country.

Prime Minister Winston Churchill tours the bomb-damaged streets of London, accompanied by his wife, Clementine. Churchill's defiance in the face of Nazi aggression helped the British endure dark days during the Battle of Britain.

his colleagues: "Send all the bloody pumps you've got; the whole bloody world's on fire."[2] Heat from the flames was so intense that it blistered paintwork on riverboat vessels moored hundreds of yards from the warehouses. By nightfall, thousands of pumps were working desperately to contain the worst of the inferno, with firemen and engines called in from across southeastern England. Some areas of the East End became virtually cut off by the fires. The flames hemmed in Silvertown—an area that was a mixture of small factories and slum houses wedged along the Thames—for hours. The firemen who were able to reach the area were unable to quench the flames properly because the main water line had been breached.

The German bombers came back on Sunday, Monday, and Tuesday. St. Katharine's dock, packed with paraffin and wax, was burned to the ground in a five-hour blaze. Flames rose 200 feet (61 m) in the air. Between September 7 and November 13, 1940, the Germans bombed the British capital almost every day with an average of 160 bombers on each occasion. More than 27,500 tons (24.9 million kg) of high explosives were dropped across London, and more incendiaries than could ever possibly be counted.

A CITY UNDER SIEGE

Before the outbreak of the war, government experts had been pessimistic about the effects of sustained bombing on civilians. Ordinary people would panic, they suggested. There would be a mass exodus from the cities as millions of people fled for their lives. Urban life would grind to a halt. In fact, little of this sort of thing happened in London. Certainly, Londoners feared for themselves, for their families, and for their property. There were incidents of panic, of looting, and of other reprehensible behavior. The surprising thing about the Blitz, however, is how quickly people adjusted to it. Life under the bombs was far from easy, but it could be sustained with some imagination and willingness to adapt. This was true of the enemy also. When Germany's cities eventually came under attack from British and American bombers later in World War II, most people accepted their lot without panicking. Far from breaking morale, bombing tended to make civilians even more determined to continue fighting. Londoners showed this "Blitz Spirit" in its finest form.

By the spring of 1941, German bombs had killed about 43,000 people across Britain, half of them in London. This was a heavy toll, without question. When one considers that the population of the United Kingdom at the time was about 48 million, however, with more than 8 million living in the capital, one can see that the chance of being killed by a German bomb was not as great as one may imagine. The Blitz's main effect on

ORDEAL BY FIRE

Millions of ordinary Britons who experienced the Blitz in 1940 were left with indelible memories of what they saw. This account was written by Doris Bennett, a young woman who was working as a telephone operator at a London Fire Brigade station on the first Saturday the German bombers attacked the British capital. The Isle of Dogs district in the East End of London where Bennett was stationed, surrounded on three sides by the River Thames, was a prime target for the Luftwaffe that day:

> That Saturday was a warm, sunny autumn day. In the late afternoon we of the Auxiliary Fire Service, stationed at the London Fire Brigade station at the bottom end of the Isle of Dogs, were standing in the station yard watching the vapor trails of aircraft high in the sky when it was suggested we might get a better view from an upstairs window.
>
> Watching from the window towards Greenwich, across the Thames, we suddenly saw aircraft approaching, quite low. . . . We watched, mesmerized, until someone said, uneasily, "I think we'd better go downstairs, these blokes look like they mean business." They did. We closed the window and were walking, unhurriedly down the stairs when suddenly came loud rushing noises and huge explosions. . . . We huddled together in a corner of the stairwell until the noises ceased, then pulled ourselves together and made our way down the rest of the stairs.
>
> We made our way to our Control Room and took our places in front of the telephones. The first call came

most people was to make their lives complicated. Bombs ruptured water and sewage mains, electricity and telephone lines, and gas pipes. They cratered roads and smashed up railroad

> very quickly. . . . Around the edges close to the river were timber yards, paint works, boiler making and engineering factories, and other factories producing jams, pickles and confectionery. Across the top of the Island were the three large West India Docks, and down the middle were the Millwall Docks, their sides lined with shipping from all over the world and their warehouses stuffed with the cargoes those ships had carried. At the bottom end of the Millwall Docks were MacDougalls flour mills, their tall silos an outstanding landmark, and highly inflammable. The Germans were well aware of this. . . .
>
> It must have been around midnight when our boss called us together and said the way things were there was no point in all of us staying on duty. . . . We collected tunics and tin hats and went to the back door to make our way across the Yard. It was after midnight and I had expected to walk out into the blackout we had grown accustomed to, but the night was as bright as day from the light of the fires all around us flickering on the walls of houses and tall buildings. . . .
>
> The shelter was made of four or five corrugated iron sections bolted together, half buried in the soil of what had been the Station garden. . . . The floor had been boarded, and kapok quilts, intended to cover engines and keep them as warm as possible in very cold weather, were spread upon the floor. We arranged them, and ourselves, not very comfortably, and tried to get some sleep. . . . *
>
> ---
> * British Broadcasting Corporation Web site, "The London Blitz," http://www.bbc.co.uk/ww2peopleswar/stories/41/a2613241.shtml.

In this 1940 photo, Londoners sleep on the platform and tracks of the Aldwych Underground Station in London during the Blitz.

tracks. Simply getting to and from work or shopping for groceries following a heavy raid could take hours because of disrupted public transport. Hundreds of unexploded bombs proved more troublesome to the authorities than bombs that actually went off. While they were being defused (a process that could take hours), entire neighborhoods had to be evacuated.

The night raids made it hard to get a good night's sleep. Tired factory workers had to haul themselves out of bed to make the trek to the air-raid shelter. Eventually, many East Enders simply began to sleep in shelters all the time. At the beginning of the Blitz, the shelters that the British government had prepared for civilians were quickly shown to be inadequate: They were small, damp, unsanitary, and vulnerable to bomb damage. Londoners took matters into their own hands and occupied stations of the subway system, the Underground, also known as the Tube, at night. At first, the authorities tried to prevent this, but soon they realized that it was a good solution to a major public safety problem. One some nights, as many as 177,000 Londoners would sleep on Tube platforms deep underground.

On September 13, 1940, Buckingham Palace was bombed for the first time. It turned out to be a huge propaganda blunder for the Germans. Queen Elizabeth was relieved: "Now I feel we can look the East End in the face."[3] Previously the government had feared that class resentment might build up among poor Londoners who thought they were bearing all the brunt of the war. Now King George VI and his family, who visited bombed-out neighborhoods to offer their sympathies, became hugely popular symbols of the British will to resist. With invasion still a very real possibility, Queen Elizabeth was asked whether the two royal princesses should be evacuated to safety in Canada. They could not leave without her, she explained, and she could not leave without the king. King George would never leave London. So that was that.

A CRUCIAL RESPITE

In his headquarters at RAF Bentley Priory on the outskirts of London, Hugh Dowding looked at the blazing city in the distance each night with greatly mixed feelings. As the leader of the RAF's main line of air defense, he felt guilty about his inability to prevent the suffering of Londoners, for whom he felt a personal responsibility. He also knew, however, that the Luftwaffe's decision to switch to city bombing at this critical moment in the Battle of Britain had granted vital breathing space to 11 Group. In early September, its airfields had

Queen Elizabeth and King George VI inspect the bomb damage at Buckingham Palace in London, after an air raid during the Blitz, in September 1940. The royal family refused to find safety elsewhere during the entire Battle of Britain.

received such a pounding that Dowding began to seriously consider withdrawing the RAF from Kent and East Sussex. Now Sir Keith Park's men were being left alone to repair the damage to their bases and return to full duty.

Also, flying to London exposed the Luftwaffe to new dangers. The great city was at the very edge of the Bf 109's range. The German fighters could operate for only a few minutes over the capital before having to turn for home. Estimating the amount of fuel in their tanks was not easy, and many pilots found themselves having to ditch in the English Channel. The bombers, meanwhile, now had a very long flight to and from their target, much of it under inadequate fighter escort. They were under scrutiny from RDF radio towers for much longer, allowing RAF controllers to dispatch intercepting Hurricanes and Spitfires with greater accuracy. Also, 12 Group at last had the time to build up its Big Wing formations properly.

Dowding suspected that the climax to the battle was coming soon. With autumn drawing in, the English Channel would not be suitable for a large-scale invasion force for much longer. Only a couple of weeks remained before the Germans must either launch Operation Sea Lion or cancel it until 1941 at the earliest. He knew that Göring would throw his maximum effort into a last-ditch attempt to break Britain before his time ran out. The moment of decision was nigh.

Invasion Thwarted

On the morning of Sunday, September 15, 1940, Sir Keith Park had a nasty shock. Over breakfast, his wife reminded him that it was her birthday. Given that the commander of Fighter Command's 11 Group had just spent the preceding two months defending Great Britain from invasion, it was perhaps forgivable that this detail had slipped his mind. Nonetheless, he apologized. It was quite all right, his wife reassured him, a large number of shot-down German aircraft that day would make the perfect birthday present.

As it turned out, Mrs. Park's birthday was not the only awkward surprise the 11 Group's leader would have that morning. When he arrived at headquarters, he discovered that Winston Churchill had chosen to stop by to view the proceedings. The prime minister was escorted up to a viewing gallery where he could watch the group controllers receive updates from RAF

Bentley Priory. Nothing, initially, was happening over southern England. The plotting boards manned by WAAFs were empty. Churchill's mood was not improved by the fact that he was forbidden to smoke while in 11 Group's headquarters and had to chew on an unlit cigar instead. Park was not having the easiest of days.

The calm over Kent would not last. By noon, at least 200 Luftwaffe aircraft were heading for London, more than three-quarters of them Bf 109 fighters. The Germans were trying to draw out the Spitfires and Hurricanes and defeat them in a climactic single combat. Within two hours, another 115 bombers and no less than 340 additional single-engine fighters joined this advance German attack group. Göring had sent up every plane he could muster in an attempt to overwhelm the British defenses. The RAF fighters rose to intercept them. Back in 11 Group headquarters, Churchill, who was usually silent during his visits, asked Park how many reserve planes and pilots Fighter Command had left that were not committed to the battle in the skies. The answer he got was simple. None, Park said.

BATTLE OF BRITAIN DAY

Park was not exaggerating. Almost every Fighter Command aircraft in southern England was scrambled into action that Sunday. As the two sides approached one another at speeds in the hundreds of miles per hour, their spirits could not have been more different. The British knew that they would be outnumbered, but since the lifting of the air raids on their bases, the RAF's pilots had been able to get some badly needed sleep and rest. They were eager to press the attack. For their part, the German crews were now despondent about their chances. Again and again, Göring had promised them that the British air force was on the brink of collapse; yet it did not collapse. Indeed, it seemed to be getting stronger. Few retained any

(continues on page 94)

ADOLF GALLAND (1912–1996)

Already one of the Luftwaffe's most experienced pilots because of his flying practice in the Spanish Civil War, Adolf Galland rose during the battle of Britain to become Germany's highest-scoring ace, ending 1940 with 57 kills to his credit. He commanded a fighter wing (Gruppe) of three Bf 109 squadrons throughout the Battle; under Galland's leadership this Gruppe, with its distinctive yellow-nosed aircraft, became respected and feared on the British side as an elite unit. Galland would lead a charmed life during World War II, surviving 705 combat missions and being shot down without serious injury four times.

Galland was the second of four sons of a bailiff, or land official, in western Germany. As a teenager, he developed an interest in flying when he joined a gliding club. In 1932, he joined Germany's commercial airline company Lufthansa as a pilot. Within a short time, however, he had been approached by one of the leaders of Germany's new Nazi government, Hermann Göring, who was trying to secretly establish an air force. Galland began to teach other future military aviators in a clandestine training program. In February 1935, Hitler openly revealed the existence of the air force (in defiance of the Versailles Treaty). A year later, Galland commanded a squadron of ground-attack biplanes sent by Hitler to Spain to assist General Francisco Franco's fascist rebels. Galland learned much in Spain about fundamental aviation tactics. He also developed an eccentric personal style, flying a plane decorated with a Mickey Mouse illustration while he himself wore swimming trunks and smoked a cigar.

At the outbreak of World War II, Galland took part in the Polish and French campaigns. On May 12, 1940, he

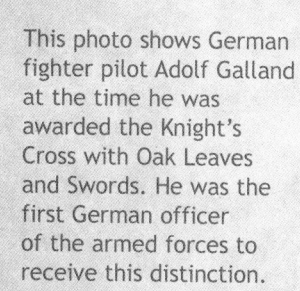

This photo shows German fighter pilot Adolf Galland at the time he was awarded the Knight's Cross with Oak Leaves and Swords. He was the first German officer of the armed forces to receive this distinction.

claimed his first aerial victory when he shot down two Hurricanes. By July, he had been placed in charge of the Luftwaffe's 26th Fighter Wing (*Jagdgeschwader* 26). JG26, as it was known for short, took part in all the great aerial battles over southern England that summer. As the battle raged, Galland was frustrated by the limitations being placed on his fighter pilots by Göring. Once, when asked by the Luftwaffe leader what his Gruppe needed most of all, Galland replied: "A squadron of Spitfires." Only Galland's high standing in the air force protected him against such insolence. By the end of 1940, he had been personally awarded by Hitler the Knight's Cross with Oak Leaves and swords, one of Germany's most prestigious military decorations.

In November 1941, Galland became the Luftwaffe's overall commander of fighters. He spent the remainder of the war trying, against increasingly desperate odds, to build

(continues)

> a strong defensive shield against the strategic bombers of the RAF and the U.S. Army Air Forces, which were pounding Germany's cities. At the end of the war, Galland surrendered to the Americans. After serving two years as a prisoner of war, he was returned to Germany, where he spent the remainder of his life as a private aviation consultant. In his final years, he became close friends with many RAF veterans who had fought against him in the Battle of Britain.

(continued from page 91)
illusions that the coming battle would be the mopping up of a broken enemy. The overconfident predictions of German intelligence reports earlier in the conflict were now replaced by in cynicism and disillusion.

It was a beautiful fall day, fine and warm with only patches of occasional clouds. The outcome of the day's combat would be decided by individual skill, not the vagaries of the weather. Soon, a continuous rolling dogfight with hundreds of aircraft on either side developed over Kent, moving slowly northwestward toward London. As one British or German squadron peeled away to refuel, another would take its place in the line of battle. By the time the Germans were approaching the outskirts of the capital, 12 Group's Big Wing, commanded by Douglas Bader, was in position. Big Wings had often failed in the past because of bad timing, much to the fury of Park; but on this occasion Bader's force arrived at exactly the right moment. Sending his Spitfires to deal with the Bf 109s, Bader ordered the Hurricanes to intercept the bombers. Soon, numerous Do 17s, He 111s, and Ju 88s were spiraling toward the ground with smoke hemorrhaging from their engines, their crews scrambling to parachute from their doomed aircraft.

A few German bombers made it as far as London, but their tight organization had been broken up and their aim was scrappy. On the long return trip through 11 Group's airspace, there was no longer any pretense of maintaining a disciplined formation; it was every plane for itself. Awaiting their squadrons' return, German observers on the French coast were horrified to see streams of aircraft filleted with British bullet holes limping eastward, some unable to maintain enough height to reach their bases and having to ditch in the sea. Back in England, the RAF pilots too were tired, but their victory was obvious. The Germans had been turned back in disarray. Mrs. Park had her birthday present.

September 15, 1940, was to become known as "Battle of Britain Day," the climax of the summer's great confrontation. Initial reports suggested that the RAF had shot down 185 enemy planes. After sober intelligence analysis had taken place, this was reduced to a more realistic 34 bombers and 26 fighters destroyed—but still, a great tally. The RAF itself had lost 25 planes, with 13 pilots killed or missing. The Germans could not afford such disproportionate casualties any longer. September 15 was the last time that Göring's air force attempted a mass daylight raid over Britain. Attacks on London at night, when the Spitfires and Hurricanes were grounded, would continue, but the Luftwaffe now had to concede the daylight skies over southern England to the RAF. Attaining air supremacy, an essential precondition for the success of Operation Sea Lion, was impossible for the foreseeable future.

A BATTLE OF MANY NATIONS

Among the RAF pilots who flew in defense of Britain on September 15 were many who were not British. Although for convenience's sake historians often refer to the "British" Royal Air Force in 1940, in fact 595 of the 2,936 aircrew officially recognized as taking some active part in the Battle of Britain were not citizens of the United Kingdom. Their participation underscores the fact that what was at stake in the skies over southern England that summer was not simply Britain's freedom, but that of the world as a whole.

THE VIEW FROM THE GERMAN SIDE

Luftwaffe pilots wrote vividly of their aerial encounters with the RAF over the skies of southern England during the Battle of Britain. First Lieutenant Gerhard Schöpfel, the second-in-command to Adolf Galland, described a dogfight that took place on August 18, 1940:

> Suddenly I found a squadron of Hurricanes below me in the usual British formation of tight threes, which were climbing in a spiral. I circled about 3,300 feet [1,005 m] above them. Then I saw a pair of Hurricanes weaving behind the formation, on guard against an attack from astern. I waited until they were curving north-westwards from Folkestone, then attacked out of the sun and below. [Schöpfel shot down the pair without alerting the other RAF planes.]
> Now I was beneath a third machine. I fired a short burst. This aircraft likewise fell apart. The British flew on, having noticed nothing. I positioned myself under a fourth machine. This time I had to get closer. When I pressed the firing button the Hurricane was so close to me that fragments from it hit my aircraft. Oil covered my cockpit so thickly that I couldn't see, and after two minutes of action I had to break off.

Second Lieutenant Karl Borris, another Bf 109 pilot, described a further encounter with Hurricanes above the White Cliffs of Dover:

Many of these non-British pilots were young men from the British Dominions and empire. There were 127 New Zealanders, 112 Canadians, 32 Australians, 25 South Africans,

> Low on our left a formation appeared, apparently enemy fighters, by the suspicious look of their flying in threes. Low on our right someone reported another formation, towards which our commander [*Kommandeur*] turned.... Ahead and beneath us flew three machines that I recognized as Hurricanes. Apparently the Kommandeur hadn't seen these, as he was watching the two big formations which were still some three miles in front of us. I dived ... 400 yards ... 300 ... 200 [366 m ... 274 ... 183]. I had the British pilot on the left in my sights. Would the other two turn on me? My concentration was stretched to the breaking point. One hundred yards ... 70 yards [91 m ... 64 m], the Hurricane grew big. Now! It swerved aside. I stopped shooting. It was on fire. I hauled my machine round in a climbing turn to rejoin my flight.
>
> In front of me a Bf 109 was firing at a Hurricane but couldn't turn as tightly as it. I side slipped down on the Hurricane ... 70 yards ... 50 [64 m ... 46]. My four machine guns hurled bullets at it. Thick black smoke and flames belched from it. I broke upwards. A little lower a Hurricane had spotted me. Climb! The British plane couldn't keep up with me. He gave up and swung away. Where were my friends? I couldn't see anything. From above and behind an airplane was hurtling towards me. In an instant I rolled onto my back and disappeared....*

*Richard Townshend Bickers, *The Battle of Britain*. London: Salamander, 1999.

as well as representatives from Jamaica, Palestine (now Israel), and Southern Rhodesia (today known as Zimbabwe). Ten men from neutral Ireland also flew with the RAF, as did seven Americans. The Americans were defying a legal restriction prohibiting any U.S. citizen from serving in the armed forces of another country; many of them had slipped across the border to Canada before coming to Britain and adopting false nationality papers. Eventually, when the United States entered the war in December 1941, these early indiscretions were forgotten and the American veterans became celebrated members of the U.S. Army Air Forces, with valuable battle lessons to teach their countrymen.

Aside from the British dominions, the second-largest contingent of foreign-born pilots came from German-occupied Europe. There were 145 Poles, 88 Czechs, 28 Belgians, and 13 Frenchmen, most of whom had already seen combat in the skies above their own countries when the Germans invaded. Dowding was initially very skeptical about their potential contribution to Fighter Command. He assumed that the language barrier would make communication between the group headquarters and the squadrons in flight confusing. As it turned out, these fears were unfounded. Two all-Polish and two all-Czech squadrons were formed. One of these—Number 303 "Kościuszko" Squadron, named for a Polish hero of the American revolutionary war who ironically fought against the British—became one of the highest-scoring RAF squadrons of the entire battle, with 44 confirmed kills. The Poles, who had bitter memories of their country's defeat in 1939, were renowned for their ferocity in combat. They often drew terrifyingly close to Luftwaffe aircraft in order to open fire at point-blank range, generating the mostly untrue rumor that they deliberately tried to ram the Germans.

INVASION POSTPONED

On September 19, four days after the great battle over London, Hitler quietly told his subordinates not to add any more vessels to the invasion fleet assembling in the English Channel ports. On October 12, he added that Germany should begin slowly winding down preparations for any immediate landing in England. Clearly, his faith in Operation Sea Lion was dwindling in the wake of Battle of Britain Day. Yet the German leader would not yet abandon the possibility of an invasion of Britain, at least in public. On November 12, he accepted that the operation would no longer take place in 1940, but he still held out the possibility that it could be revived the following year and told his army, air force, and navy commanders to keep that contingency in mind.

In truth, however, Hitler's attention had already drifted elsewhere. Never very keen on the war with Britain in the first place, he now resolved to ignore it entirely and to concentrate his thoughts on a far more alluring prize: the Soviet Union. On December 18, he warned his closest advisers in a top-secret directive that the real German target for 1941 would be the Soviet Union. The Blitz on London and other British cities would be merely a cheap and useful distraction for the world while the Germans moved their forces eastward.

Back in London, Churchill, Dowding, Park, and the pilots of the RAF did not realize it, but the Battle of Britain was over. They had won.

Their Finest Hour

Decisive battles usually end with a climactic flourish, a critical moment of conflict on the field, after which the two sides disengage, one in triumph, the other in desperate flight. The Battle of Britain had no such neat ending. The date that was later chosen by the RAF to mark the official end of the battle was October 31, but this was as arbitrary a choice as July 10 had been for its start. Peace did not suddenly descend on southern England on November 1, 1940. Although the intensity of air fighting declined, the Luftwaffe continued to launch "nuisance" raids on Kent and Sussex during the day. At night, its bombers still dropped their high explosives and incendiaries on London and other cities. Throughout the winter of 1940, pilots and aircrew on both sides died; ordinary British men, women, and children sheltered in fear from the Blitz.

In fact, the postwar decision that the Battle of Britain had officially ended on October 31 generated some controversy. Archibald McKellar was the first RAF pilot to shoot down a German aircraft over the United Kingdom during World War II. He went on to fight throughout the Battle of Britain, and his total of 17 kills—including five Bf 109s on a single day—was among the highest single score of any of the aces on the British side. On November 1, McKellar's Hurricane was shot down over Kent and he was killed. Although McKellar received the posthumous award of the Distinguished Service Order, one of the RAF's highest awards for gallantry, he was not included on the Battle of Britain roll of honor because he had been killed a few hours after the battle had ended. His name is not among those listed at the RAF memorial in London's Westminster Abbey. Not surprisingly, McKellar's relatives were incensed that he had been excluded from the ranks because of a technicality. The British Air Ministry was unmoved; the Battle of Britain had to officially end sometime, even if this caused a few injustices to happen. It is hard to imagine that McKellar's fellow pilots would have seen it the same way.

The vagueness of the Battle of Britain's end, however, prompts another, bigger question: Can a battle really be said to have been decisive if it is not even clear exactly when it was over? What exactly *did* the Battle of Britain decide, if anything?

VICTORY?

Because Hitler had called off Operation Sea Lion indefinitely and the Luftwaffe had withdrawn from its daylight campaign over southern England, the Germans were judged to have lost the Battle of Britain. That said, it is important to understand that the British position remained desperate in the winter of 1940. German planes continued to harass civilians by night. The worst nights of the Blitz were still to come, in fact. On the evening of November 14, 1940, Luftwaffe bombers launched a surprise attack on Coventry in the English Midlands. More than 4,000 homes and three-quarters of the city's factories were destroyed; Coventry's famous medieval cathedral burned to the ground. Liverpool, Portsmouth, Hull, Clydebank, and Belfast were among the many towns across the United Kingdom heavily damaged by German raiders over the winter.

London's worst nights lay ahead also. On December 29, in the so-called Second Great Fire of London, the ancient center of the British capital was burned out. Thanks to the heroic efforts of London's firefighters, St. Paul's Cathedral, at the heart of the city, was saved, but the photos of its great dome surrounded by smoke and flames that December evening have become permanently associated with the suffering of ordinary Londoners during the war. Perhaps the most devastating raid of all would not come until May 10, 1941, exactly one year after Churchill had been made prime minister. More than 1,300 Londoners were killed that day, the highest death toll of the Blitz. The chamber of the House of Commons, Churchill's political home for the past 40 years, was destroyed.

In other respects, too, Britain's position immediately after the Battle of Britain was gloomy. Germany and its allies controlled almost the whole of the European mainland. When British troops tried to intervene in Greece to prevent a German invasion, they were thrown out in disarray. At sea, the Kriegsmarine's submarines, or U-boats, were sinking British merchant vessels faster than they could be replaced. As an island nation, Britain relied absolutely on its naval lines of communication and supply. If these were broken, the country could be starved into submission.

Diplomatically, Britain had few friends left to call upon for help. The Dominions of Canada, Australia, New Zealand, and South Africa gave vital support, as did the colonies of the far-flung empire in India, Africa, and Asia. The United States, however, the most powerful and important country of all, remained neutral. Ordinary Americans had come to

St. Paul's Cathedral rises above the smoke and flames on one of the worst nights of bombing experienced in Britain, December 29, 1940. German aircraft had dropped more than 10,000 incendiary bombs on London, but the landmark church and its dome somehow remained untouched.

increasingly sympathize with Britain's plight, moved as they had been by the Blitz broadcasts of CBS journalist Edward R. Murrow. President Roosevelt, who was eager to help Churchill if he could, had been able to provide some practical assistance via the Lend-Lease Act—a program under which the United States supplied the United Kingdom and other Allied nations with war materials between 1941 and 1945.

Americans, however, were still not ready to take the final step to war. Memories of the bloodshed of World War I were still too strong. Churchill made eloquent appeals to Roosevelt for military intervention, but without the backing of American public opinion the U.S. president could only go so far.

So as the spring of 1941 beckoned, it is little wonder that many on both sides were girding themselves for a second round of the Battle of Britain. The RAF had had an opportunity to rest and reequip, but so had the Luftwaffe. Operation Sea Lion had only been postponed, not canceled. The British had avoided defeat in 1940. Would they be able to do so again against an even better prepared enemy?

THE WAR BECOMES GLOBAL

World War II was about to take a completely different direction. As Hitler had revealed to a few of his chosen inner circle, by the winter of 1940, he was already thinking of new conquests in Eastern Europe. Hitler had long regarded Joseph Stalin's Union of Soviet Socialist Republics (USSR) as Nazi Germany's true enemy, and his pact with Stalin prior to the invasion of Poland had been nothing more than a temporary expedient while he dealt with his opponents in the West. Now that France was occupied, and Britain was too weak to seriously interfere with Germany's plans, it was time to march on Moscow.

On June 22, 1941, more than 4.5 million German and allied troops invaded the Soviet Union. The initial results were as spectacular as the Blitzkriegs against Poland and

France had been. By September, the Germans had advanced hundreds of miles into the interior of western Russia. By the beginning of December, they were barely 30 miles (48.2 km) from the Soviet capital. The foul Russian weather, however, was interfering with their operations. German troops sank into the autumn mud and then froze in the winter snow. Soviet troops then mounted a successful counterattack and saved Moscow from defeat.

Halfway around the world, the United States had also become involved in the war. On December 7, 1941, just as German troops were falling back from the fringes of Moscow, the U.S. Pacific Fleet anchored at its Hawaiian base at Pearl Harbor was attacked by surprise by Japanese fighters and bombers. The Japanese, frustrated at American demands that they withdraw from an invasion of China, had decided to finish off their rivals in a lightning attack. The Japanese marched into the U.S.-held Philippine Islands and British colonies in Hong Kong and Malaya (today, Malaysia). Hitler, ecstatic at the initial success of his Japanese allies and eager to turn his own U-boats against the Americans in the Atlantic, declared war on America also. Churchill had at last gotten what he wanted most of all, albeit in a quite unexpected way.

Although many battlefield defeats were still to come for the British, Americans, and Soviets, the war had in fact reached its turning point. Germany and Japan would prove to be no match for the combined manpower and economic might of the three main Allies fighting as one. By mid-1943, the Germans were in full retreat across the USSR. The following year, on June 6, 1944—D-Day—Allied forces landed in Normandy in France to begin the liberation of Western Europe. Surrounded on all sides, the Germans shrank back to their own frontier; on April 30, 1945, with Soviet troops just yards away from his underground headquarters in Berlin, Hitler committed suicide.

(continues on page 108)

CHURCHILL PRAISES "THE FEW"

On August 16, 1940, Winston Churchill visited 11 Group's operations room at RAF Uxbridge to watch the progress of that day's combat between the British and German air forces. Afterward, greatly moved by the bravery he witnessed, he decided to speak about the heroism of the RAF's pilots in his next war report to Parliament. The speech he gave on August 20 has become famous for its stirring use of the term *the Few* to describe the embattled but defiant Fighter Command aircrew. Churchill ended his account of events by emphasizing the relationship between Great Britain and the United States:

> Almost a year has passed since the war began, and it is natural for us, I think, to pause on our journey at this milestone and survey the dark, wide field. . . .
>
> Hitler is now sprawled over Europe. Our offensive springs are being slowly compressed, and we must resolutely and methodically prepare ourselves for the campaigns of 1941 and 1942. Two or three years are not a long time, even in our short, precarious lives. They are nothing in the history of the nation, and when we are doing the finest thing in the world, and have the honour to be the sole champion of the liberties of all Europe. . . . One of the ways to bring this war to a speedy end is to convince the enemy, not by words, but by deeds, that we have both the will and the means, not only to go on indefinitely but to strike heavy and unexpected blows. . . .
>
> We cannot tell what lies ahead. It may be that even greater ordeals lie before us. We shall face whatever is coming to us. We are sure of ourselves and of our cause and that is the supreme fact which has emerged in these months of trial. . . .

The great air battle which has been in progress over this Island for the last few weeks has recently attained a high intensity. . . . The gratitude of every home in our Island, in our Empire, and indeed throughout the world, except in the abodes of the guilty, goes out to the British airmen who, undaunted by odds, unwearied in their constant challenge and mortal danger, are turning the tide of the world war by their prowess and by their devotion. Never in the field of human conflict was so much owed by so many to so few.

All hearts go out to the fighter pilots, whose brilliant actions we see with our own eyes day after day; but we must never forget that all the time, night after night, month after month, our bomber squadrons travel far into Germany, find their targets in the darkness by the highest navigational skill, aim their attacks, often under the heaviest fire, often with serious loss, with deliberate careful discrimination, and inflict shattering blows upon the whole of the technical and war-making structure of the Nazi power. . . .

There is one direction in which we can see a little more clearly ahead. We have to think not only for ourselves but for the lasting security of the cause and principles for which we are fighting and of the long future of the British Commonwealth of Nations. . . . The two great organisations of the English-speaking democracies, the British Empire and the United States, [are becoming] somewhat mixed up together in some of their affairs for mutual and general advantage.

For my own part, looking out upon the future, I do not view the process with any misgivings. I could not stop it if I wished; no one can stop it. Like the Mississippi, it just keeps rolling along. Let it roll. Let it roll on full flood, inexorable, irresistible, benignant, to broader lands and better days.*

---

* Winston Churchill, "The Few," House of Commons, August 20, 1940. http://www.winstonchurchill.org/learn/speeches/speeches-of-winston-churchill/1940-finest-hour/113-the-few.

Troops from the 48th Royal Marines land on Juno Beach, in Normandy, France, during D-Day, on June 6, 1944. The D-Day landings signaled the beginning of the end for Nazi Germany—and the return of British and Allied troops to France for the first time since the Battle of Dunkirk.

(continued from page 105)

A few days later, Germany surrendered unconditionally. On August 15, Japan, now in an equally hopeless position, also capitulated. World War II was over.

THE BATTLE OF BRITAIN IN HISTORY

It is only as part of this bigger context, then, that the significance of the Battle of Britain can really be seen. In the short term, the outcome of the battle was more of a stalemate than a victory. By the winter of 1940, the Germans could not subdue

Britain, but the British had no realistic way of defeating the Germans either. Neither side could knock out the other nor be knocked out itself.

Had this situation continued unchanged for another year or more, it is likely that the Germans, with all the resources of occupied Europe to draw on, would have prevailed in the end. That, however, would have meant Hitler staying patient, and patience was not one of the German dictator's strong points. Unable to achieve a quick victory, Hitler's attention wandered to the vast and distant USSR. It was a fateful and, for the Nazis, catastrophic decision.

The Battle of Britain was decisive to the outcome of World War II, then, not because it ended the war but because it *kept the war going* at a time when Germany's enemies were at their weakest and most divided. Had Hitler successfully neutralized the British in 1940, either by outright invasion or merely by forcing on them a humiliating peace, it is hard to see how the war could have ever been won by the Allies. Beginning with the invasion of the Soviet Union, the entire character of the war changed.

More than 20 million Soviet citizens died in the conflict against Germany. Their victory was a tribute to the bravery and sacrifice of the people of the USSR. Practical assistance from Britain and the United States, however, was also critical to that victory. Without the lifeline that ran through the United Kingdom and its overseas colonies, none of this aid would have gotten to Stalin's forces. The Germans would likely have taken Moscow in 1942 or 1943.

As for the United States, its economic strength and resources were considerable, but mounting a liberation of Western Europe directly from its eastern Atlantic coast, without the advantage of the British Isles as a base, would have been next to impossible. For one thing, the U.S. Army Air Forces, operating from 3,000 miles (4,828 km) away, would never have been able to secure crucial air supremacy over the invasion beaches.

At best, the United States would have had to retreat behind its ocean frontiers. In the long term, with Germany and Japan effectively controlling the whole of Europe, Asia, and Africa, America would likely have been doomed.

When Churchill said of the RAF's pilots that "never in the field of human conflict was so much owed by so many to so few," he was exactly right. The victory over the skies of southern England during the "Spitfire summer" of 1940 was far more significant than merely foiling the German plan for an invasion of Britain. It saved the world from Nazi tyranny. The young men of Fighter Command had little inkling at the time of the weight of responsibility that rested on their shoulders. The 544 of them who did not survive the battle died not only in the service of their country, but also in the greater cause of a free and just world. Their names are rightly revered today in the annals of heroism.

CHRONOLOGY

1933 Adolf Hitler becomes chancellor of Germany.

1936 Hitler renounces the disarmament clauses of the Treaty of Versailles and begins rearming the German armed forces, creating the Luftwaffe.

1938 Germany annexes Austria; later, after last-minute negotiations in Munich, Britain and France agree to also allow Germany to take over the western border region of neighboring Czechoslovakia.

1939 **September 1** Germany invades Poland.

September 3 Britain and France declare war on Germany, marking the outbreak of World War II in Europe.

1940 **May 10** Germany begins its major offensive in the West by invading France, Belgium, and the Netherlands. In London, Winston Churchill becomes British prime minister.

May 26 Surrounded at the French port of Dunkirk, the British Expeditionary Force begins evacuation back to England.

June 10 Italy declares war on Britain and France.

June 25 France surrenders to Germany.

July 10 The Luftwaffe's first major attack on an English Channel convoy marks the official beginning of the Battle of Britain.

July 16 Hitler orders his military commanders to begin planning for Operation Sea Lion, an invasion of southern England.

August 13 "Eagle Day." The Luftwaffe begins its major attacks on radar installations and Royal Air Force (RAF) airfields.

August 20 Winston Churchill makes his famous speech praising the heroism of "the Few."

August 31 With six of its seven major airfields in southeastern England out of action, the RAF endures one of its worst days of the battle, losing 65 fighters.

September 7 The Luftwaffe switches tactics and begins the wholesale bombing of London. British military leaders put troops on full alert, warning that invasion may be imminent.

September 15 "Battle of Britain Day." After suffering heavy losses, the Luftwaffe abandons daylight bombing of London.

TIMELINE

1933
Adolf Hitler becomes Chancellor of Germany

1940
May 26 Surrounded at the French port of Dunkirk, the British Expeditionary Force begins evacuation back to England

1933

1940

1939
September 3 Britain and France declare war on Germany, marking the outbreak of World War II in Europe

July 10 The Luftwaffe's first major attack on an English Channel convoy marks the official beginning of the Battle of Britain

July 16 Hitler orders his military commanders to begin planning for Operation Sea Lion, an invasion of southern England

Chronology

October 31 The official end of the Battle of Britain (though the Luftwaffe continues to bomb London and other British cities at night).

November 12 Hitler postpones Operation Sea Lion until 1941 at the earliest.

1941   **June 22** Germany invades the USSR.

December 7 The United States enters the war when its naval base at Pearl Harbor, Hawaii, is attacked by Germany's ally Japan.

1944   **June 6** American, British, and Canadian troops invade France on D-Day.

1945   **April 30** Hitler commits suicide in his Berlin bunker.

1940
September 7 The Luftwaffe switches tactics and begins the wholesale bombing of London
September 15 "Battle of Britain Day." After suffering heavy losses, the Luftwaffe abandons daylight bombing of London

1941
December 7 The United States enters the war when its naval base at Pearl Harbor, Hawaii, is attacked by Germany's ally Japan

1945

October 31 The official end of the Battle of Britain
November 12 Hitler postpones Operation Sea Lion until 1941 at the earliest

1945
May 8 Germany surrenders, and the Allies celebrate V-E Day, marking victory in Europe

May 8 Germany surrenders, and the Allies celebrate V-E Day, marking victory in Europe.

August 15 Japan surrenders, signing formal surrender documents on September 2.

NOTES

CHAPTER 1
1. Winston Churchill, "Their Finest Hour," House of Commons, June 18, 1940. http://www.winstonchurchill.org/learn/speeches/speeches-of-winston-churchill/1940-finest-hour/122-their-finest-hour.
2. Air Power Australia. http://www.ausairpower.net/Quotes.html.

CHAPTER 3
1. *Time*, August 16, 1982. http://www.time.com/time/magazine/article/0,9171,950756,00.html.
2. Churchill, "Their Finest Hour."

CHAPTER 4
1. The Battle of Britain Historical Society Web site, "Luftwaffe Aircraft and Pilot Losses, August 1940," http://www.battleofbritain1940.net/document-41.html.
2. Steven Bungay, *The Most Dangerous Enemy: A History of the Battle of Britain*. London: Aurum Press, 2000, p. 107.

CHAPTER 5
1. Jean Edward Smith, *FDR*, New York: Random House, 2008, p. 772.
2. Bungay, *The Most Dangerous Enemy*, p. 148.

CHAPTER 6
1. Richard Overy, *Battle of Britain: The Myth and the Reality*. London: Penguin, 2000, p. 83.
2. The Battle of Britain Historical Society Web site, "Wednesday, September 4th, 1940," http://www.battleofbritain1940.net/0034.html.

CHAPTER 7
1. Peter Stansky, *The First Day of the Blitz*. New Haven, Conn.: Yale University Press, 2007, p. 38.
2. Philip Ziegler, *London at War*. New York: Knopf, 1995, p. 113.
3. Ibid., p. 121.

BIBLIOGRAPHY

BOOKS

Bickers, Richard Townshend. *The Battle of Britain.* London: Salamander, 1999.

Bungay, Steven. *The Most Dangerous Enemy: A History of the Battle of Britain.* London: Aurum Press, 2000.

Dahl, Roald. *Going Solo.* London: Penguin, 1986.

Evans, Ray. *Before the Last All Clear.* New York: Morgan James, 2008.

Hillary, Richard. *The Last Enemy.* London: Macmillan, 1942.

Overy, Richard. *Battle of Britain: The Myth and the Reality.* London: Penguin, 2000.

Smith, Jean Edward. *FDR.* New York: Random House, 2008.

Stansky, Peter. *The First Day of the Blitz.* New Haven, Conn.: Yale University Press, 2007.

Ziegler, Philip. *London at War.* New York: Knopf, 1995.

WEB SITES

Air Power Australia
   http://www.ausairpower.net

The Battle of Britain Historical Society
   http://www.battleofbritain1940.net

BBC: The People's War
   http://www.bbc.co.uk/ww2peopleswar

The Churchill Centre and Museum at the Churchill War Rooms, London
   http://www.winstonchurchill.org

The Churchill Society
   http://www.churchill-society-london.org.uk

World War II Database
   http://ww2db.com

FURTHER RESOURCES

BOOKS

Bishop, Patrick. *Fighter Boys: The Battle of Britain, 1940.* New York: Penguin, 2004.

Crook, David. *Spitfire Pilot.* London: Grub Street, 2008.

Deighton, Len. *Fighter: The True Story of the Battle of Britain.* London: Pimlio, 2008.

Fisher, David E. *A Summer Bright and Terrible: Winston Churchill, Lord Dowding, Radar, and the Impossible Triumph of the Battle of Britain.* Berkeley, Calif.: Counterpoint, 2006.

Kershaw, Alex. *The Few: The American "Knights of the Air" Who Risked Everything to Fight in the Battle of Britain.* New York: De Capo Press, 2006.

Korda, Michael. *With Wings Like Eagles: A History of the Battle of Britain.* New York: HarperCollins, 2009.

Priestley, Chris. *Battle of Britain: A Second World War Spitfire Pilot, 1939–1941.* New York: Scholastic, 2008.

Wellum, Geoffrey. *First Light.* Hoboken, N.J.: Wiley, 2003.

WEB SITES

Battle of Britain Day by Day
   http://battleofbritainblog.com/

The Spitfire Site
   http://spitfiresite.com/

PICTURE CREDITS

PAGE

9: Infobase Learning
12: The Stapleton Collection / The Bridgeman Art Library
21: Paul Popper/Popperfoto/ Getty Images
25: Hulton Archive/Getty Images
27: Hulton Archive/Getty Images
36: Keystone/Hulton Archive/ Getty Images
39: Paul Popper/Popperfoto/ Getty Images
45: © INTERFOTO/Alamy
52: © World History Archive/ Alamy
59: Hulton Archive/Getty Images
71: Paul Popper/Popperfoto/ Getty Images
73: William Vanderson/Hulton Archive/Getty Images
82: Topical Press Agency/Hulton Archive/Getty Images
86: © NMPFT/Daily Herald Archive/SSPL/The Image Works
88: Fox Photos/Hulton Archive/ Getty Images
93: © DIZ Muenchen GmbH, Sueddeutsche Zeitung Photo/Alamy
103: © Daily Mail/Rex/Alamy
108: Hulton Archive/Getty Images

INDEX

A
Adlertag, 60–61, 64, 65
aircraft. *See also Specific aircraft*
   earliest military uses of, 16–17
   of Luftwaffe, 44–47
   of Royal Air Force, 49–53
   Wielún and, 18–19
airfields, battle for, 64–65
amputations, 70
Anglo-French expeditionary force, 35–36
appeasement, policy of, 28–29
Austria, annexation of by Germany, 30, 80–81

B
B-17 "Flying Fortress," 48
Bader, Douglas, 68–69, 70–71, 94
bailiffs, 92
Battle of Britain Day, 95
Belgium, 37–38
Bennett, Doris, 84–85
Bentley Priory, 54, 78–79
Berlin, bombing of, 77
Bf 109 planes, 45, 48, 96–97
Bf 110 planes, 45–46, 57, 60, 88–89
Big Wings, 68–69, 71, 89
Black Saturday, 79
Blitz on London, 79–87, 99
Blitzkrieg, 32
Boeing B-17 "Flying Fortress," 48
Boer War, 35
Bolshevik Revolution, 20
bomb shelters, 86–87
Bomber Command, 48
Borris, Karl, 96–97
Bread convoy, 8

Buckingham Palace, bombing of, 87, 88
burn injuries, 74–75, 76
businessmen, Hitler and, 24

C
Chain Home, 53–54, 61
Chamberlain, Neville, 27, 28–29, 35, 36, 37
channel battles, 57
Churchill, Randolph, 34
Churchill, Winston
   appointment of as prime minister, 37
   Battle of Dunkirk and, 42
   on consequences of failure in Battle of Britain, 13–14
   on Munich Agreement, 29
   overview of, 34–35, 36
   Phony War and, 33
   praise of RAF pilots by, 106–107, 110
   visit of to Fighter Command 11 Group headquarters, 90–91
Coastal Command, 48
Colditz castle, 71
communists, Hitler and, 24
convoys, raids on, 57
Coventry, bombing of, 102
Czechoslovakia, 27, 28, 30

D
Dahl, Roald, 10–11
D-Day, 105, 108
death toll
   of Battle of Britain, 13, 100
   from Blitz, 83–84
   of World War I, 19

Denmark, 34–35
detection, radar and, 63
Doppler shift, 63
Dowding, Hugh
    Blitz on London and, 87–88
    caution of, 57
    overview of, 58–60
    radar and, 53
    RAF Fighter Command and, 49
    tactics of RAF and, 68–69
Dowding System, 53–54, 59, 61
Dunkirk, Battle of, 38–39, 42, 55

E

Eagle Day, 60–61, 64, 65
English Channel, 40–41, 43–44. *See also* Operation Sea Lion
equipment
    Dunkirk and, 38–39, 55
    Home Guard and, 55
    of Luftwaffe, 44–48
    Poland and, 31–32
    of Royal Air Force, 49–53
evacuation, Operation Pied-Piper and, 50–51
Evacuee Distribution Centre, 51
Evans, Ray and Frank, 50–51

F

fairies, 60
false alarms, 54
Fascist Europe, map of, 9
fatigue, 68, 74
Fighter Command, 49, 53–54, 59–60, 106–107, 110
fires
    injuries from, 74–75, 76
    in London, 79–83
Fiske, William, 14–15
Flying Fortress planes, 48
formations, importance of, 65
France
    Battle of Dunkirk and, 38–39
    Holland and Belgium and, 37–38
    invasion of Poland and, 32–33
    Munich Agreement and, 28–29
    surrender of, 42
fuel, quality of, 52

G

Galland, Adolf, 92–94
Germany
    attacks on Holland and Belgium and, 37–38
    Battle of Dunkirk and, 38–39, 42
    disagreements about tactics of, 69, 72
    equipment of, 32, 44–48
    Operation Sea Lion and, 42, 43–44, 95, 98–99, 101
    overestimation of combat kills by, 65–66, 76
    reasons for defeat of Poland by, 31–33
    rise of Hitler and Nazi party in, 24–27, 30
    World War I and, 19–21, 24
ghosts, 60
Göring, Hermann
    Adolf Galland and, 92
    Operation Sea Lion and, 44, 56–57
    overview of, 46–47
    tactics of Luftwaffe and, 69, 72
Great Britain
    after Battle of Britain, 102–104
    Battle of Dunkirk and, 38–39, 42
    equipment of, 49–53
    Holland and Belgium and, 37–38
    Home Guard and, 55–56
    invasion of Poland and, 32–33
    Munich Agreement and, 28–29

Index

Great Depression, 24, 25
Greece, 102
gross domestic product, of Germany, 26

H
Hardest Day, 64
Harrow, bombing of, 77
"Harry Clampers" sky, 7
Hawker Hurricane planes
   losses of, 64–65
   overview of, 49–51, 53
Hellfire Corner, 57
Higgs, Tom, 11–13
Hillary, Richard, 74–75
Hindenberg, Paul von, 23
Hitler, Adolf
   death of, 23, 105
   lack of patience of, 76–77, 109
   Operation Sea Lion and, 40–41, 98–99, 101
   overview of, 22–23
   rise of, 24–27, 30
Hitler, Alois, 22
Holland, 37–38
Home Guard, 55–56
Hurricane planes
   losses of, 64–65
   overview of, 49–51, 53
hyperinflation, 25

I
incendiary bombs, 79
Isle of Dogs district, 84–85

J
Japan, 105
Jericho's Trumpets, 18
Jerome, Jennie, 34
Jews, Hitler and, 24
JG26 group, 93
Junkers Ju 87 dive-bombers
   limitations of, 61, 64

   Wielún and, 18–19, 32, 46

K
Kennedy, Joseph P., 56
Kent, attacks on airfields in, 64–65
kills, overestimation of, 65–66, 76
knighthood, 71, 81

L
Leigh-Mallory, Trafford, 59–60, 68–69, 71
Lend-Lease Act, 104
Local Defence Volunteers (LDV), 55–56. *See also* Home Guard
London, bombing of, 79–87, 100, 102, 103
Luftflotten, 44–45
Lufthansa, 92
Luftwaffe, overview of, 44–48
Luxembourg, 38

M
maps, of Fascist Europe, 9
McCarthy, Joseph, 81
McIndoe, Archibald, 74–75, 76
McKellar, Archibald, 101
McNeil, Olive, 79
Mein Kampf (Hitler), 23
Messerschmitt Bf 109 planes, 45, 48, 96–97
Messerschmitt Bf 110 planes, 45–46, 57, 60, 88–89
Millionaire's Squadron, 15
Mitchell, R.J., 49
morphine, 47
Munich Agreement, 27, 28–29
Murrow, Edward R., 80–81, 104

N
Namibia, 46
National Socialist German Workers Party (NSDAP), 23, 24–26, 46–47

Index

Nazi party, 23, 24–26, 46–47
Netherlands, 37–38
Norway, 33–37
NSDAP. *See* Nazi party
nuisance raids, 100

O
Olympics, 14–15
Operation Pied-Piper, 50–51
Operation Sea Lion, 42, 56–57, 95, 98–99, 101

P
Panzer divisions, 32
Paris, fall of, 42
Park, Keith
   bombing of London and, 88–89
   disagreements about tactics of RAF and, 68–69
   RAF Fighter Command and, 49
   visit of Churchill to headquarters and, 90
Pearl Harbor attack, 105
Phony War, 33–37
Pied-Piper, Operation, 50–51
pilots
   overview of, 72–76
   praise of by Churchill, 106–107, 110
plastic surgery, 74–75, 76
Poland
   invasion of by Germany, 19–21, 23, 30
   reasons for fall of, 31–33
Pollick, Michael, 62–63

R
radar, 53–54, 62–63. *See also* Radio Direction Finding stations
Radio Direction Finding (RDF) stations, 8, 53–54, 61
Raeder, Erich, 44
RAF. *See* Royal Air Force
ranging, radar and, 63
RDF stations. *See* Radio Direction Finding stations
reconnaissance, use of airplanes in, 16
Red Baron (Manfred von Richthofen), 46
Red Scare, 81
reincarnation, 60
religion, 60
reparation payments, 24
Reynaud, Paul, 38
Ribbentrop, Joachim von, 27
Richthofen, Manfred von, 46
Roosevelt, Franklin Delano, 56, 80, 104
Royal Air Force (RAF)
   disagreements about tactics of, 68–69, 72
   Douglas Bader and, 70–71
   overview of, 48–53
   Roald Dahl and, 10–11
Royal Flying Corps, 58

S
Schöpfel, Gerhard, 96
Sea Lion, Operation, 42, 56–57, 95, 98–99, 101
Second Great Fire of London, 102
shelters, bombing and, 86–87
Sitzkrieg, 33–37
Slave Treaty, 24
sled racing, 14
socialists, Hitler and, 24
Somme, Battle of, 21
Soviet Union, 32, 99, 104–105, 109
Spanish Civil War, 44, 92
Spitfire planes
   losses of, 64–65
   overview of, 49–51, 53
St. Paul's Cathedral, 102, 103

Index

Stalin, Joseph, 32, 104
Stuka dive-bombers
　limitations of, 61, 64
　Wielún and, 18–19, 32, 46
subway, as bomb shelter, 86–87
Sudetenland, annexation of by Germany, 27, 28
suicide
　of Göring, 47
　of Hitler, 23, 105
Supermarine Spitfire planes
　losses of, 64–65
　overview of, 49–51, 53
Surrey Commercial Dock, 81
swarm formation, 65, 72

T

tanks, Germany and, 32
technology, Poland and, 31–32
Third Reich, 26
total war, 19–20
training, lack of for pilots, 73
traitors, Hitler and, 24

U

U-boats, 102
Underground, use of as bomb shelter, 86–87
United Kingdom
　after Battle of Britain, 102–104
　Battle of Dunkirk and, 38–39, 42
　equipment of, 49–53
　Holland and Belgium and, 37–38
　Home Guard and, 55–56
　invasion of Poland and, 32–33
　Munich Agreement and, 28–29
United States
　impacts of Battle of Britain on, 109–110
　neutrality of, 102–104
　Pearl Harbor and, 105
　volunteers from, 14–15, 98

V

Versailles, Treaty of, 20–21, 24, 26–27, 92
Vic formation, 65
volunteers
　American, 14–15, 98
　British, 55–56

W

WAAF. *See* Women's Auxiliary Air Force
Wall Street crash of 1929, 23
Weygand, Maxime, 56
Wielún, bombing of, 18–19, 32
Wilhelm II (German Emperor), 20
Wilhelmina (Queen of Netherlands), 37–38
Wilson, Woodrow, 20
windshields, 48
Women's Auxiliary Air Force (WAAF), 61
World War I, 19–21, 24, 35
Wright Brothers, 15–16

ABOUT THE AUTHOR

ALAN ALLPORT grew up in Whiston, England, and moved to the United States in 1994. He received a doctorate in history from the University of Pennsylvania in 2007 and currently teaches at Syracuse University. He lives in DeWitt, New York, with his wife and their children, Thomas and Katharine. In addition to penning numerous books for Chelsea House, he is the author of *Demobbed: Coming Home after the Second World War*, published by Yale University Press in 2009.